MARK T. TOTTEN

9-19-85

D0064898

YOUR ATTITUDE:
Key to Success

YOUR ATTITUDE:
Key to Success

BY

JOHN MAXWELL

HERE'S LIFE PUBLISHERS, INC.
SAN BERNARDINO, CALIFORNIA 92402

Your Attitude:
Key To Success

©1984 by John Maxwell

Published by
HERE'S LIFE PUBLISHERS, INC.
P.O. Box 1576
San Bernardino, California 92402

International Standard Book Number: 0-89840-067-8
Library of Congress Catalogue Card Number: 84-047800
HLP Product No. 950816

Printed in the United States of America.
Second printing, September, 1984.

Unless otherwise indicated, Scripture quotations are from the
New American Standard Bible, ©The Lockman Foundation
1960, 1962, 1963, 1971, 1972, 1973, 1975, and are used by permission.

YOUR ATTITUDE: KEY TO SUCCESS *is dedicated to Dr. Tom Phillippe, Sr. He is my friend, a co-laborer in the Gospel and an example of proper attitude living.*

Contents

ACKNOWLEDGEMENTS

Thanks for this book must be expressed to my parents, Melvin and Laura Maxwell, for providing a home life that was accented with healthy attitudes for living. Positive attitudes which are more caught than taught surrounded me the day I was born.

My wife, Margaret, provided wise counsel and our children, Elizabeth and Joel Porter, gave me many illustrations. The Maxwell family is trying to live the principles of this book.

Appreciation is also to be given to my staff at Skyline Wesleyan Church for their input into this book. Their insights, questions and suggestions highlighted many Tuesday staff meetings. Barbara Brumagin, my personal secretary, especially followed through on this project.

"Thank you" to Paul Nanney for his friendship and exciting flying experiences that added to this book.

Foreword

Dear Reader:

I wish I had some way of force-feeding this unique and powerful book down everyone's soul to nourish and nurture their attitudinal growth process.

Of course, I'm biased and wholly prejudiced about the author because he is my balcony-person friend, my spiritual conscience and my pastor. However, I have the unique advantage of listening to and reading many communicators from all over the world so I know a good one when I see or hear one. And John Maxwell is the very best!

John's book zeroes in realistically from the opening concept—a person's attitude dictates his performance—clear through to his extremely practical ways to change not only our own attitudes but also even those of the people around us.

I have never had an encounter with this godly man, whether personal and private or with others as a member of his congregation, without being changed dramatically by his attitude. He is a *natural* to write on this incredibly important subject.

In his book, John's hand stretches out beyond the pages, grabs us, and, by way of inspired teaching, shows us amazing practical concepts. And, as usual, he continually turns us in the Lord's direction—so we end up falling in love with Christ afresh.

Watch John Maxwell, for he is one of God's choicest servants and one of the clearest communicators of our day. God has enormous plans for him and you and I will reap the rich overflow of this man's life.

—*Joyce Landorf*

SECTION I
THE CONSIDERATION OF YOUR ATTITUDE

1

It's a Bird ...
No, it's a Plane ...
No, it's an Attitude

Have this attitude in yourselves which was also in Christ Jesus (Philippians 2:5).

IT WAS A BEAUTIFUL DAY in San Diego, and my friend, Paul, wanted to take me for a ride in his airplane. Being new to Southern California, I decided to see our new home territory from a different perspective.

We sat in the cockpit as Paul completed his instrument checks. Everything was A-Okay, so Paul revved the engines and we headed down the runway. As the plane lifted off, I noticed the nose was higher than the rest of the airplane. I also noticed that while the countryside was truly magnificent, Paul continually watched the instrument panel.

Since I was not a pilot, I decided to turn the pleasure ride into a learning experience. "All those gadgets," I began, "What do they tell you? I notice you keep looking at that one instrument more than the others. What is it?"

"That's the attitude indicator," he replied.

"How can an airplane have an attitude?"

"In flying, the attitude of the airplane is what we call the position of the aircraft in relation to the horizon."

By now my curiosity had been aroused, so I asked him to explain more.

"When the airplane is climbing it has a nose-high attitude because the nose of the airplane is pointed above the horizon."

"So," I jumped in, "when the aircraft is diving you would call that a nose-down attitude."

"That's right," my instructor continued. "Pilots are concerned about attitude of the airplane because that dictates its performance."

"Now I can understand why the attitude indicator is in such a prominent place on the panel," I replied.

Paul, sensing I was an eager student, continued, "Since the performance of the airplane depends on its attitude, it is necessary to change the attitude in order to change the performance."

He demonstrated this by bringing the aircraft into a nose-high attitude. Sure enough, the plane began to climb and speed

decreased. He changed the attitude, and that changed the performance!

Paul concluded the lesson by saying, "Since the attitude of the airplane determines its performance, instructors now teach 'attitude flying.'"

That conversation triggered my thinking concerning people's attitudes. Doesn't an individual's attitude dictate his performance? Does he have an "attitude indicator" that continually evaluates his perspective and achievements in life? What happens when the attitude is dictating undesirable results? How can the attitude be changed? And, if the attitude changes, what are the ramifications to other people around him?

My friend, Paul, had an instructor's manual on "Attitude Flying," the relationship between the aircraft's attitude and its performance. We, too, have been given a handbook for attitude living ... the Bible.

The apostle Paul, when writing to the church at Philippi, placed before those Christians an attitude indicator. "Have this attitude in yourselves which was also in Christ Jesus" (Philippians 2:5).

Christ gives us a perfect example to follow. His high standard was not given to frustrate us, but to reveal areas in our lives that need improvement. Whenever I study Philippians 2:3-8, I am reminded of the healthy attitude qualities that Jesus possessed.

He was selfless. "Do nothing from selfishness or empty conceit, but with humility of mind let each of you regard one another as more important than himself; do not merely look out for your own personal interests, but also for the interests of others" (vs. 3,4).

He was secure. "Who, although He existed in the form of God, did not regard equality with God a thing to be grasped, but emptied Himself, taking the form of a bond-servant, and being made in the likeness of men" (vs. 6,7).

He was submissive. "And being found in appearance as a man, He humbled Himself by becoming obedient to the point of death, even death on a cross" (v. 8).

Paul says that these qualities were exhibited in the life of Christ because of His attitude (v. 5). He also says that we can

13

have this same attitude in our lives. We have a visual example of a Christian attitude and we are also encouraged to attain it.

Paul states in Romans 12:1,2, "I urge you therefore, brethren, by the mercies of God, to present your bodies a living and holy sacrifice, acceptable to God, which is your spiritual service of woship. And do not be conformed to this world, but be transformed [How?] by the *renewing of your mind*, that you may prove what the will of God is, that which is good and acceptable and perfect."

The result of a "renewed mind" or a changed attitude is to prove and fulfill God's will. Again we see that the attitude dictates the performance.

Recently I preached a message from Psalm 34 entitled, "How to Face Fear." David was lonely, fearful and frustrated in a cave surrounded by the enemy when he wrote this comforting message. The opening of the chapter enables the reader to see the reason for David's success even when surrounded by problems.

David's Three-Fold Process of Praise:

1. PRAISE BEGINS WITH THE WILL (v. 1).

"I will bless the Lord at all times; His praise shall continually be in my mouth." His attitude reflects a determination to rejoice regardless of the situation.

2. PRAISE FLOWS TO THE EMOTION (v. 2).

"My soul shall make its boast in the Lord." Now, David is praising the Lord not only because it's right but also because he feels like it.

3. PRAISE SPREADS TO OTHERS (v. 2,3).

"The humble shall hear it and rejoice. O magnify the Lord with me, and let us exalt his name together." David demonstrates that the desired performance "praise" begins with an attitude that is determined to do it. The conclusion of the chapter records David's triumphant "The Lord redeems the soul of His servants; and none of those who take refuge in Him will be condemned."

Attitude living, like attitude flying, says "my attitude dictates my performance." That "canopy" represents a lot of ground to cover in one book. We'll need to examine:

What is an attitude, and why is it important?

What are the necessary ingredients for a high-performance

attitude?

What causes an attitude to become negative, disappointing?

How can a wrong attitude that is working against us be turned around to work for us?

Along the way we will discover the attitude indicators revealed in persons described in the Bible, the best handbook on attitude performance available since God Himself gave it to us. Obviously, this will not be the last word on this critical subject. But I hope it will be an enlightening word to those who understand the importance of the attitude. I pray it will be helpful to those who want to change.

Attitude Application:

Take a few minutes before proceeding and ask yourself the following questions:

Have I checked my attitude lately?

How would I rate my attitude?

Never been better _____

Never been worse _____

Nose-up _____

Nose down _____

What is an attitude indicator (something which reflects my perspective) in my life?

2

THE ATTITUDE—WHAT IS IT?

"A person cannot travel within and stand still without."
—James Allen

THE HIGH SCHOOL BASKETBALL team I played for was not having a good season, and one day the coach had one of those team meetings in which every player was quiet and listening. The coach continually stressed the relationship between the team's attitude and the win-loss record. I can still hear his words, "Fellows, your abilities say 'win,' but your attitudes say 'lose.'"

Parents are called to school for a conference concerning their child. The issue? Timmy, a fifth-grader, has failing grades and is causing a disturbance among his classmates. His aptitude tests show he is intellectually capable, yet he is failing miserably. The teacher suggests he has a "bad attitude."

A member of the congregation is being discussed in a pastoral staff meeting. Constantly recurring in the conversation is the phrase, "She has a terrific attitude."

Hardly a day passes without the word "attitude" entering a conversation. It may be used as a complaint or a compliment. It could mean the difference between a promotion or a demotion. Sometimes we sense it, other times we see it. Yet, it is difficult to explain.

The attitude is an inward feeling expressed by behavior. That is why an attitude can be seen without a word being said. Haven't we all noticed "the pout" of the sulker, or "the jutted jaw" of the determined? Of all the things we wear, our expression is the most important.

My daughter Elizabeth has brought much joy to our family, yet her personality at times tends to be melancholic. When she

16

feels that way, her face does not express happiness. My wife, Margaret, recently bought Elizabeth a figurine that says, "Put on a happy face." It is a reminder that our expressions usually reflect our inward feelings.

The Bible teaches us " . . . God sees not as man sees, for man looks at the outward appearance, but the Lord looks at the heart" (I Samuel 16:7). "The heart is more deceitful than all else and is desperately sick; who can understand it?" (Jeremiah 17:9). These statements express our inability to know for sure what emotions are going on inside someone else. Yet, while we refrain from judging others by their outward expressions, many times the outward actions become a "window to the soul." A person who gives "a look that kills," probably is not inwardly singing "Something Good is Going to Happen to You."

Acts 20 gives the account of Paul stopping at Miletus and calling for the Ephesian elders. These men gathered and listened to Paul's farewell address. The future was uncertain and their leader declared, "And now, behold, bound in spirit, I am on my way to Jerusalem, not knowing what will happen to me there, except that the Holy Spirit solemnly testifies to me in every city, saying that bonds and afflictions await me" (vs. 22,23).

Paul exhorted these church leaders to watch over the work that he had begun. Inwardly they were moved with compassion for the man who had discipled them. Their attitudes of love resulted in a touching display of affection. "And when he had said these things, he knelt down and prayed with them all. And they began to weep aloud and embraced Paul, and repeatedly kissed him, grieving especially over the word which he had spoken, that they should see his face no more. And they were accompanying him to the ship" (vs. 36-38).

Since an attitude often is expressed by our body language and by the looks on our faces, it can be contagious. Have you noticed what happens to a group of people when one person, by his expression, reveals a negative attitude? Or have you noticed the lift you receive when a friend's facial expression shows love and acceptance?

David's music and presence encouraged a troubled King Saul. Scripture tells us "the Spirit of the Lord departed from Saul, and an evil spirit from the Lord terrorized him" (I Samuel 16:14). The king's men were told to find someone who could lift their ruler's spirit. They brought David into the palace and "Saul loved him greatly .... And Saul sent to Jesse, saying, 'Let David now stand before me; for he has found favor in my sight.' So it came about whenever the evil spirit from God came to Saul, David would take the harp and play it with his hand; and Saul would be refreshed and be well, and the evil spirit would depart from him" (vs. 21-23). Sometimes the attitude can be masked outwardly, and others who see us are fooled. But usually the cover-ups will not last long. There is that constant struggle as the attitude tries to wiggle its way out.

My father enjoys telling the story of the four-year-old boy who had one of those trouble-filled days. After reprimanding him, his mother finally said to him, "Son, you go over to that chair and sit on it now!" The little lad went to the chair, sat down, and said, "Mommy, I'm sitting on the outside, but I'm standing up on the inside." Have you ever said that to God? We all have experienced the inner conflict similar to the one expressed by Paul in Romans 7, "For the good that I wish, I do not do; but I practice the very evil that I do not wish ... but I see a different law in the members of my body, waging war against the law of my mind, and making me a prisoner of the law of sin which is in my members. Wretched man that I am! Who will set me free from the body of this death? Thanks be to God through Jesus Christ our Lord! So then, on the one hand I myself with my mind am serving the law of God, but on the other, with my flesh the law of sin" (vs. 19, 23-25).

Sound familiar? Whenever a sincere Christian asks me to help him with his spiritual walk I always talk about obedience. The simplicity of "Trust and Obey," that great hymn by James H. Sammis, points to the importance of our obedient attitude to our spiritual growth.

"While we walk with the Lord in the light of His Word,
What a glory He sheds on our way!
While we do His good will, He abides with us still,
And with those who will trust and obey.
Trust and obey for there's no other way,
To be happy in Jesus, but to trust and obey."

During a time of congregational renewal at Skyline Wesleyan Church, where I am the senior pastor, my heart was challenged with the words of Mary, the mother of Jesus, who said, "Whatever He [Jesus] says to you, do it." I shared with my congregation this thought of obedience drawn from the story of Jesus' miracle at the wedding in Cana (John 2:1-8):

Whatever Jesus says to you, do it, even though . . .

1. You are not in the "right place" (v. 2).

They were at a wedding and not a church when Jesus performed the miracle. Some of God's greatest blessings will be at "other places" if we will be obedient to Him.

2. You have a lot of problems (v. 3).

They had run out of wine! Too many times our problems drive us away from Jesus instead of to Him. Christian renewal begins when we focus on God's power and not our problems.

3. You are not encouraged (v. 4).

Jesus said to those at the wedding, "My hour has *not yet* come." Instead of being discouraged by these words, Mary laid hold of the possibility of a miracle.

4. You have not walked with Him very long (v. 5).

The servants who obeyed Jesus had just met Him, and the disciples had just started following the Lord, yet they were expected to obey Him.

5. You have not seen Him work miracles in your life.

This was our Lord's first miracle. The people in this situation had to obey Him without His having a previous track record.

6. You don't understand the entire process.

From this biblical story we can draw out a definition for obedience. It is listening to the words of Jesus and doing His will. Inward obedience provides outward growth.

Psychologist/philosopher James Allen states, "A person cannot travel within and stand still without." Soon what is happening within us will effect what is happening without. A hardened attitude is a dreaded disease. It causes a closed mind and a dark future. When the attitude is positive and conducive to growth, the mind expands and the progress begins.

What is an attitude?

It is the "advance man" of our true selves.
Its roots are inward but its fruit is outward.
It is our best friend or our worst enemy.
It is more honest and more consistent than our words.
It is an outward look based on past experiences.
It is a thing which draws people to us or repels them.
It is never content until it is expressed.
It is the librarian of our past;
It is the speaker of our present;
It is the prophet of our future.

Attitude Application:

Choose a friend and evaluate his attitude. Write down several words that describe it. What is his performance indicator as a result of that attitude? Now, do this for yourself.

3

THE ATTITUDE—WHY IS IT IMPORTANT?

"Do you feel the world is treating you well? If your attitude toward the world is excellent, you will receive excellent results. If you feel so-so about the world, your response from that world will be average. Feel badly about your world, and you will seem to have only negative feedback from life."

—*John Maxwell*

WE LIVE IN A world of words. Attached to these words are meanings that bring varied responses from us. Words such as happiness, acceptance, peace and success describe what each of us desires. But there is one word that will either heighten the possibility of our desires being fulfilled or prevent them from becoming a reality within us.

While leading a conference in South Carolina I tried the following experiment. To reveal the significance of this word, I read the previous paragraph and asked, "What word describes what will determine our happiness, acceptance, peace and success?" The audience began to express words such as job, education, money, time. Finally someone said "attitude." Such an important area of their lives was a "second thought." Our attitude is the primary force that will determine whether we succeed or fail.

For some, attitude presents a difficulty in every opportunity; for others it presents an opportunity in every difficulty. Some climb with a positive attitude, while others fall with a negative perspective. The very fact that the attitude "makes some" while "breaking others" is significant enough for us to explore its importance. Studying the major statements listed in this chapter will highlight this truth to us.

Attitude Axiom #1:
Our attitude determines our approach to life.

The story of the two buckets underlines this truth. One bucket was an optimist, and the other was a pessimist.

"There has never been a life as disappointing as mine," said the empty bucket as it approached the well. "I never come away from the well full, but what I return again empty."

"There has never been such a happy life as mine," said the full bucket as it left the well. "I never come to the well empty, but what I go away again full."

Our attitude tells us what we expect from life. If our "nose" is pointed up, we are taking off; if it is pointed down, we may be headed for a crash.

One of my favorite stories is about a grandpa and grandma who visited the grandchildren. Each afternoon, grandpa would lie down for a nap. One day, as a practical joke, the kids decided to put Limburger cheese in his moustache. Quite soon he awoke sniffing. "Why, this room stinks," he exclaimed as he got up and went out into the kitchen. He wasn't there long until he decided that the kitchen smelled too, so he walked outdoors for a breath of fresh air. Much to grandpa's surprise, the open air brought no relief, and he proclaimed, "The whole world stinks!" How true that is to life. When we carry "Limburger cheese" in our attitudes, the whole world smells bad.

One of the valid ways to test your attitude is to answer this question: "Do you feel your world is treating you well?" If your attitude toward the world is excellent, you will receive excellent results. If you feel so-so about the world, your response from the world will be average. Feel badly about your world, and you will seem to have only negative feedback from life.

Look around you. Analyze the conversations of people who lead unhappy, unfulfilled lives, and you will find they are crying out against society, which they feel is out to get them and to give them a lifetime of trouble, misery and bad luck. Sometimes the prison of discontent has been built by their own hands.

The world doesn't care whether we free ourselves from this prison or not. It marches on. Adopting a good, healthy attitude toward life does not affect society nearly as much as it affects us. The change cannot come from others. It must come from us. The apostle Paul had a terrible background to overcome. He told Timothy that he was the "chief of sinners." But after his conversion he was infused with desire to know Christ in a greater way. How did he fulfill this desire? Not by waiting for someone else to assist him. Neither did he look backward and whine about his terrible past. Paul diligently "pressed on to lay hold of Jesus." His singleness of purpose caused him to state, "But one thing I do: forgetting what lies behind and reaching forward to what lies ahead, I press on toward the goal for the prize of the upward call of God in Christ Jesus" (Philippians 3:13, 14).

We are individually responsible for our view of life. The Bible says, " . . . whatever a man sows, this he will also reap" (Galatians 6:7). Our attitude and action toward life helps determine what happens to us.

It would be impossible to estimate the number of jobs which have been lost, the number of promotions missed, the number of sales not made and the number of marriages ruined by poor attitudes. But almost daily we witness jobs that are held but hated, and marriages that are tolerated but unhappy, all because people are waiting for others, or the world, to change, instead of realizing that they are responsible for their behavior. God is sufficient to give them the desire to change, but the choice to act upon that desire is theirs.

It is impossible for us to tailor-make all situations to fit our lives perfectly. But it is possible to tailor-make our attitudes to fit! The apostle Paul beautifully demonstrated this truth while he was imprisoned in Rome. He certainly had not received a "fair shake." The atmosphere of his confinement was dark and cold. Yet, he writes to the church at Philippi brightly declaring, "Rejoice in the Lord *always*; again I will say rejoice!" (Philippians 4:4, emphasis mine). Notice that the confined man was telling carefree people to rejoice! Was Paul losing his mind? No. The secret is found late in the same chapter. Paul states, "Not that I speak from want; for I have *learned* to be content in whatever circumstances I am. I know how to get along with humble means and I also know how to live in prosperity; in any and every circumstance I have *learned* the secret of being filled and going hungry, both of having abundance and suffering need" (vs. 11,12, emphasis mine). The ability to tailor-make his attitude to his situations in life was learned behavior. It did not come automatically. The behavior was learned and a positive outlook became natural. (I will talk more about this learned behavior in Section IV, "The Changing of Your Attitude.") Paul repeatedly teaches us by his life that man helps create his environment—mental, emotional, physical and spiritual—by the attitude he develops.

Attitude Application:

Circle the number that most closely reveals your attitude toward life:

1   "Make the World Go Away"
2   "Raindrops Keep Falling on my Head"
3   "I Did It My Way"
4   "Oh, What a Beautiful Morning"

Attitude Axiom #2:
Our attitude determines our relationships with people.

The Golden Rule: "Therefore whatever you want others to do for you, do so for them" (Matthew 7:12).

This axiom takes on a higher significance when, as Christians, we realize that effective ministry to one another is based on relationships.

The model of ministry (as I understand ministry) is best captured in John 13. Christ and His disciples are gathered in the upper room.

The components of Christ's model of ministry are:
(1) men with whom He had shared all arenas of life;
(2) an attitude and demonstration of servanthood;
(3) an all-encompassing command of relational love. ("By this all men will know you are My disciples.")

An effective ministry of relating to others must include all three of these biblical components. No single methodology (preaching, counseling, visitation) will effectively minister to all the needs all the time. It takes a wise combination of many methods to reach the needs of people. And, the bridge between the gospel remedy and people's needs is leadership based on relationship.

24

John 10:3-5 gives a view of relational leadership through the imagery of a shepherd leader: "The sheep hear his voice and come to him; and he calls his own sheep by name and leads them out. He walks ahead of them; and they follow him, for they recognize his voice. They won't follow a stranger but will run from him, for they do not recognize his voice" (Living Bible).

These verses further delineate the components of relational leadership:.

1. relationship to the point of instant *recognition* (He calls His own sheep by name);
2. established relationship built on *trust* (His sheep hear his voice and come to Him);
3. *modeled* leadership (He walks ahead of them; and they follow Him).

Yet, establishing such relationships is difficult. People are funny. They want a place in the front of the bus, the back of the church and the middle of the road. Tell a man there are 300 billion stars, and he will believe you. Tell that same man that a bench has just been painted, and he has to touch it to be sure.

People are frustrating at times.They show up at the wrong place at the wrong time for the wrong reason. They are always interesting but not always charming. They are not always predictable because they have minds of their own. You can't get along with them, and you can't make it without them. That's why it is essential to build proper relationships with others in our crowded world.

The Stanford Research Institute says that the money you make in any endeavor is determined only 12% by knowledge and 87½% by your ability to deal with people.

$$87.5\% \text{ people knowledge}$$
$$+ \qquad\qquad = \text{success}$$
$$12.5\% \text{ product knowledge}$$

That is why Teddy Roosevelt said, "The most important single ingredient to the formula of success is knowing how to get along with people."

"I will pay more for the ability to deal with people than any other ability under the sun," asserted John D. Rockefeller.

J. Paul Getty, when asked what was the most important quality for a successful executive, replied, "It doesn't make much difference how much other knowledge or experience an executive possesses; if he is unable to achieve results through people, he is worthless as an executive."

When the attitude we possess places others first and we see people as important, then our perspective will reflect their viewpoint, not ours. Until we walk in the other person's shoes and see life through another's eyes, we will be like the man who angrily jumped out of his car after a collision with another car. "Why don't you people watch where you're driving?" he shouted wildly. "You're the fourth car I've hit today!"

A few years ago I was traveling in the South and stopped at a service station for some fuel. It was a rainy day, yet the station workers were diligently trying to take care of the customers. I was impressed by the first-class treatment and fully understood the reason when I read this sign on the front door of the station:

WHY CUSTOMERS QUIT

1% die
3% move away
5% other friendships
9% competitive reasons (price)
14% product dissatisfaction

BUT ...

68% quit because of an attitude of indifference toward them by some employee!

In other words, 68% quit because the workers did not have a customer mind-set working for them.

Usually the person who rises within an organization has a good attitude. The promotions did not give that individual an outstanding attitude, but an outstanding attitude resulted in promotions. A recent study by Telemetrics International concerned those "nice guys" who had climbed the corporate ladder. A total of 16,000 executives were studied. Observe the difference between executives defined as "high achievers" (those who generally have a healthy attitude) and "low achievers" (those who generally have an unhealthy attitude):

High achievers tended to care about people as well as profits; low achievers were preoccupied with their own security.

High achievers viewed subordinates optimistically; low achievers showed a basic distrust of subordinates' abilities.

High achievers sought advice from their subordinates; low achievers didn't.

High achievers were listeners; low achievers avoided communication and relied on policy manuals.

In 1980-81 I took on a rather ambitious project, which included teaching and leading fifteen pastors and their congregations to become growing, vibrant churches. One of my favorite responsibilities was to speak in a Sunday service and recruit workers for that particular church. Right before the "enlisting service," I would ask the pastor how many people he thought would come forward, sign a card and enlist in evangelism and discipleship. I would watch the pastor slowly calculate the "who woulds" and the "who would nots." After receiving the carefully chosen number, I would announce, "More than that number will sign up." Why could I say that? Did I know his people and his situation better than he did? Of course not. What I did know was that the pastor had mentally placed his people into slots and "knew" how they would react during the service. Since I did not know the congregation, my attitude was open and positive toward all of them. I treated the listeners as if they all would respond, and most did! All fifteen pastors guessed lower than the actual laity response.

A negative past experience sometimes paralyzes our thinking and our attitude. A man unable to find his best saw suspected his neighbor's son, who was always tinkering around with woodworking. During the next few days everything that the young man did looked suspicious, the way he walked, the tone of his voice and his gestures. But when the older man found the saw behind his own workbench, where it had fallen when he accidently knocked it off the bench, he no longer saw anything suspicious in his neighbor's son.

Attitude Application:

Challenge: For one week treat every person you meet, without a single exception, as the most important person on earth. You will find that they will begin treating you the same way.

Attitude Axiom #3:
Often our attitude is the only difference
between success and failure.

History's greatest achievements have been made by men who excelled only slightly over the masses of others in their fields.

This could be called the principle of the slight edge. Many times that slight difference was attitude. The former Israeli Prime Minister Golda Meir underlined this truth in one of her interviews. She said, "All my country has is spirit. We don't have petroleum dollars. We don't have mines or great wealth in the ground. We don't have the support of a world-wide public opinion that looks favorably on us. All Israel has is the spirit of its people. And if the people lose their spirit, even the United States of America cannot save us." This great lady was saying,

$$Resources - Right\ Attitude = Defeat$$
$$Right\ Attitude - Resources = Victory$$

Below I've listed resources that enable a person to achieve success. Beside this list write down some of your other blessings. Read them when you are losing that slight edge.

health	experiences	connections
friends	family	aptitude
money	attitude	goals

Certainly aptitude is important to our success in life. Yes, success or failure in any undertaking is caused more by mental attitude than by mental capacities. I remember times when Margaret, my wife, would come home from teaching school frustrated because of modern education's emphasis on aptitude instead of attitude. She wanted the kids to be tested on A.Q. (attitude quotient) instead of just the I.Q. (intelligence quotient). She would talk of kids whose I.Q. was high, yet their performance was low. There were others whose I.Q. was low but their performance was high.

As a parent, I hope my children have excellent minds, and an outstanding attitude. But if I had to choose in an "either-or" situation, without hesitation I would want their A.Q. to be high.

A Yale University President some years ago gave this advice to a former president of Ohio State, "Always be kind to your A and B students. Someday one of them will return to your campus as a good professor. And also be kind to your C students. Some day one of them will return and build a two-million dollar science laboratory."

A Princeton Seminary professor discovered that the spirit of optimism really does make a difference. He made a study of great preachers across the past centuries. He noted their tremendous varieties of personalities and gifts. Then he asked the question, "What do these outstanding pulpiteers all have in common besides their faith?" After several years of searching he found the answer. It was their cheerfulness. In most cases, they were happy men.

There is very little difference in people, but that little difference makes a big difference. The little difference is attitude. The big difference is whether it is positive or negative. Nowhere is this principle better illustrated than in the story of the young bride from the East who, during a recent war, followed her husband to a U.S. Army camp on the edge of the desert in California.

Living conditions were primitive at best, and her husband had advised against her move, but she wanted to be with him. The only housing they could find was a run-down shack near an Indian village. The heat was unbearable in the daytime—115° in the shade. The wind blew constantly, spreading dust and sand all over everything. The days were long and boring. Her only neighbors were Indians, none of whom spoke English. When her husband was ordered farther into the desert for two weeks of maneuvers, loneliness and the wretched living conditions got the best of her. She wrote to her mother that she was coming home. She couldn't take it any more.

In a short time she received a reply which included these two lines, "Two men looked through prison bars, one saw mud, the other saw stars." She read the lines over and over again and began to feel ashamed of herself. And she didn't really want to leave her husband. All right, she thought, she'd *look* for the stars. In the following days she set out to make friends with the Indians, asking them to teach her weaving and pottery. At first they were distant, but as soon as they sensed her genuine in-

29

terest, they returned her friendship. She became friendly with their culture and history—in fact, everything about them. As she began to study the desert, it too changed from a desolate, forbidding place to a marvelous thing of beauty.

She had her mother send her books. She studied the forms of the cacti, the yuccas and the Joshua trees. She collected sea shells that had been left there millions of years ago when the sands had been an ocean floor. Later, she became such an expert on the area that she wrote a book about it.

What had changed? Not the desert; not the Indians. Simply by changing her own attitude, she had transformed a miserable experience into a highly rewarding one.

Attitude Application:

There is very little difference in people, but that little difference makes a big difference. That difference is attitude. Think of something that you desire. What attitude will you need to get it or achieve it?

Attitude Axiom #4:
Our attitude at the beginning of a task will affect its outcome more than anything else.

Coaches understand the importance of their team's having the right attitude before facing a tough opponent. Surgeons want to see their patients mentally prepared before going into surgery. Job-seekers know that their prospective employer is looking for more than just skills when they apply for work. Public speakers want a conducive atmosphere before they communicate to their audience. Why? Because the right attitude in the beginning insures success at the end. You are acquainted with the saying, "All's well that ends well." An equal truth is, "All's well that begins well."

One of the key principles I teach when leading evangelism conferences is the importance of our attitude when witnessing to others. Most of the time it is the way we present the gospel, rather than the gospel itself, that offends people. Two people can share the same news with the same person and receive different results. Why? Usually the difference is in the attitude of the person sharing. The eager witness says to himself, "People are hungry for the gospel and desirous of a positive change in their lives." The reluctant witness says to himself, "People are not interested in spiritual things and don't want to be bothered." Those two attitudes will not only determine the number of attempts made in witnessing (can you guess which one will witness?), but also will determine the results if they both share the same faith.

As an American statesman, Hubert H. Humphrey was admired by millions. His bubbly enthusiasm was contagious. When he died I cut out one of his quotes from a newspaper article about him. It was written to his wife, on his first trip to Washington, D.C., in 1935. "I can see how someday, if you and I just apply ourselves and make up our minds for bigger things, we can some day live here in Washington and probably be in government, politics, or service. Oh gosh, I hope my dream comes true; I'm going to try anyhow." With that type of attitude he couldn't fail!

Most projects fail or succeed before they begin. A young mountain climber and an experienced guide were ascending a high peak in the Sierras. Early one morning the young climber was suddenly awakened by a tremendous cracking sound.

He was convinced that the end of the world had come. The guide responded, "It's not the end of the world, just the dawning of a new day." As the sun rose, its heat was merely hitting the ice and causing it to melt.

Many times we have been guilty of viewing our future challenges as the sunset of life rather than the sunrise of a bright new opportunity.

For instance, there's the story of two shoe salesmen who were sent to an island to sell shoes. The first salesman, upon arrival, was shocked to realize that no one wore shoes. Immediately he sent a telegram to his home office in Chicago saying, "Will return home tomorrow. No one wears shoes."

The second salesman was thrilled by the same realization. Immediately he wired the home office in Chicago saying, "Please send me 10,000 shoes to sell. Everyone here needs them."

Attitude Application:

Why not write down a project that you have neglected because of an unhealthy attitude toward it? Read this axiom

31

again and again, then list all the positive benefits that will be received from the completion of your project. Remember, "All's well that begins well." Raise the level of your attitude!

Attitude Axiom #5:
Our attitude can turn our problems into blessings.

In *Awake, My Heart,* my friend, J. Sidlow Baxter, writes, "What is the difference between an obstacle and an opportunity? Our attitude toward it. Every opportunity has a difficulty and every difficulty has an opportunity" (Grand Rapids, Michigan: Zondervan Publishing House, 1960, p.10).

A person with an outstanding attitude, when confronted with a difficult situation, makes the best of it while he gets the worst of it. Life can be likened to a grindstone. Whether it grinds you down or polishes you depends upon what you are made of.

While attending a conference of young leaders I heard this statement: "No society has ever developed tough men during times of peace." Adversity is prosperity to those who possess a great attitude. Kites rise against, not with, the wind. When the adverse wind of criticism blows, allow it to be to you what the blast of wind is to the kite—a force against it that lifts it higher. A kite would not fly unless it had the controlling tension of the string that ties it down. It is equally true in life.

When Napoleon's school companions made sport of him because of his humble origin and poverty, he devoted himself entirely to his books. Quickly rising above his classmates in scholarship, he commanded their respect. Soon he was regarded as the brightest in the class.

If the germ of the seed has to struggle to push its way up through the stones and hard sod, to fight its way up to the sunlight and air and then to wrestle with the storm, snow and frost, the fiber of its timber will be all the tougher and stronger.

Few people knew Abraham Lincoln until the great weight of the Civil War showed his character.

Robinson Crusoe was written in prison. John Bunyan wrote *Pilgrim's Progress* in the Bedford jail. Sir Walter Raleigh wrote *The History of the World* during a 13-year imprisonment. Luther translated the Bible while confined in the castle of Wartburg. For 20 years Dante, author of *The Divine Comedy*, worked in exile and under the sentence of death. Beethoven was almost totally deaf and burdened with sorrow when he produced his greatest works.

When God wants to educate a man, he does not send him to the school of graces, but to the school of necessities. Through the pit and the dungeon Joseph came to the throne. Moses tended sheep in the desert before God called him for service. Peter, humbled and broken by his denial of Christ, heeded the command to "Feed my sheep." Hosea loved and cared for an unfaithful wife out of obedience to God.

In the Chinese language, whole words are written with a symbol. Often two completely unlike symbols, when put together, have a meaning different from their two separate components. An example is the symbol of "man" and that of "woman." When combined, they mean "good."

The same is true of dreams and problems. As the answers always lie in the questions, so the opportunities of life lie directly in our problems. Thomas Edison said, "There is much more opportunity than there are people to see it."

Great leaders emerge when crises occur. In the lives of people who achieve, we read repeatedly of terrible troubles which force them rise above the commonplace. Not only do they find the answers, but they discover a tremendous power within themselves. Like a ground swell far out in the ocean, this force within explodes into a mighty wave when circumstances seem to overcome. Then out steps the athlete, the author, the statesman, the scientist or the businessman. David Sarnoff said, "There is plenty of security in the cemetery; I long for opportunity."

We will know our attitude is on the right track when we are like the small businessman whose clothing store was threatened with extinction. A national chain store had moved in and acquired all the properties on his block. This one particular businessman refused to sell. "All right then, we'll build around you and put you out of business," the new competitors said. The day came when the small merchant found himself hemmed in with a new department store stretching out on both sides of his little retail shop. The competitors' banners announced, "Grand Opening!" The merchant countered with a banner stretching across the entire width of his store. It read, "Main Entrance."

Attitude Application:

List two problems that are presently a part of your life. Besides the two problems write down your present reactions to them. Are they negative? Your challenge: Discover at least three possible benefits from each problem. Now attack the problem with your eyes on the benefits, not the barriers.

Attitude Axiom #6:
Our attitude can give us an uncommonly positive perspective.

The result of that truth: the accomplishment of uncommon goals. I have keenly observed the different approaches and results achieved by a positive thinker and by a person filled with fear and apprehension.

Example: when Goliath came up against the Israelites, the soldiers all thought, "He's so big we can never kill him." David looked at the same giant and thought, "He's so big I can't miss."

Example: when you go to a shopping mall or any public place that contains a lot of cars and people, do you start at the farthest point of the parking lot and work your way toward the building, or drive to the front, assuming someone will be pulling out so you can pull in? If you operate from a positive perspective in life you will always go to the front. One time I had a friend ask me why I always assumed a close parking space would be available. My answer: "The odds are that a person coming out of the store has been in there the longest. Since that individual arrived at the store the earliest, he parked the closest." When they pull out, I drive in and give them a friendly wave. It's the least I can do for a person who has saved my parking space.

Moody Bible Institute President George Sweeting, in his sermon entitled "Attitude Makes the Difference," tells about a Scotsman who was an extremely hard worker and expected all the men under him to be the same. His men would tease him, "Scotty, don't you know that Rome wasn't built in a day?" "Yes," he would answer, "I know that. But I wasn't

34

foreman on that job."

The individual whose attitude causes him to approach life from an entirely positive perspective is not always understood. He is what some would call a "no limit person." In other words, he doesn't accept the normal limitations of life like most people. He is unwillling to accept "the accepted" just because it is accepted. His response to self-limiting conditions will probably be a "why?" instead of an "okay." He has limitations in his life. His gifts are not so plentiful that he cannot fail. But he is determined to walk to the very edge of his potential or the potential of a project before he accepts defeat.

He is like the bumblebee. According to a theory of aerodynamics, as demonstrated through wind tunnel tests, the bumblebee should be unable to fly. Because of the size, weight and shape of his body in relationship to the total wing spread, scientifically, flying is impossible. The bumblebee, being ignorant of scientific theory, goes ahead and flies anyway, and makes honey every day.

This mind-set allows a person to start each day with a positive disposition, like the elevator operator on Monday morning. The elevator was full and the man began humming a tune. One passenger seemed particularly irritated by the man's mood and snapped, "What are you so happy about?" "Well, sir," replied the man happily, "I ain't never lived this day before!"

Asked which of his works he would select as his masterpiece, architect Frank Lloyd Wright, at the age of 83, replied, "my next one."

The future not only looks bright when the attitude is right, but also the present is much more enjoyable. The positive person understands that the journey is as enjoyable as the destination.

One day a man was watching two masons working on a building. He noticed that one worker continually frowned, groaned and cursed his labors. When asked what he was doing, he replied, "Just piling one stone on top of another all day long until my back is about to break." The other mason whistled as he worked. His movements were swift and sure and his face was aglow with satisfaction. When asked what he was doing, he replied, "Sir, I'm not just making a stone wall, I'm helping

35

to build a Cathedral."

A friend of mine in Ohio drove for an interstate trucking company. Knowing the hundreds of miles he logged weekly, I once asked him how he kept from getting extremely tired. "It's all in your attitude," he replied. "Some drivers 'go to work' in the morning but I 'go for a ride in the country.'" That kind of positive perspective gives him the "edge" on life.

Attitude Application:

Notice the limitations that you or your friends accept today. With each limitation example ask the question, "Why?" Example: "Why did I choose a parking space far away without checking up close first?" Make a mental note to become a "no limit person" each time you ask the question, "why?"

Attitude Axiom #7
Our attitude is not automatically good just because we are Christians.

It is noteworthy that the seven deadly sins (pride, covetousness, lust, envy, anger, gluttony and sloth) are all matters of attitude, inner spirit and motives. Sadly, many carnal Christians carry with them inner spirit problems. They are like the elder brother of the prodigal son, thinking they do everything right. He chose to stay home with the father. No way was he

FROM TUESDAY MORNING WILL BE OKAY BY HOWARD PARIS, PUBLISHED BY TYNDALE HOUSE PUBLISHERS, INC., © 1977. USED BY PERMISSION.

going to spend his time sowing wild oats. Yet, when the younger brother came back home, some of the elder brother's wrong attitudes began to surface.

First came a feeling of self-importance. The elder brother was out in the field doing what he ought to do, but he got mad when the party began at home. He didn't get mad because he didn't like parties. I know he liked parties, because he complained to his father that he would never let him throw one!

That was followed by a feeling of self-pity. The elder brother said, "Look! For so many years I have been serving you, and I have never neglected a command of yours; and yet you have never given me a kid, that I might be merry with my friends; but when this son of yours came, who has devoured your wealth with harlots, you killed the fatted calf for him" (Luke 15:29-30).

Often we overlook the true meaning of the story of the prodigal son. We forget that we have not one but two prodigals. The younger brother is guilty of the sins of the flesh, whereas the elder brother is guilty of the sins of the spirit (attitude). When the parable closes, it is the elder—the second prodigal—who is outside the father's house.

In Philippians 2:3-8, Paul talks about the attitudes we should possess as Christians: "Do nothing from selfishness or empty conceit, but with humility of mind let each of you regard one another as more important than himself; do not merely look out for your own personal interests, but also the interests of others. Have this attitude in yourselves which was also in Christ Jesus, who, although He existed in the form of God, did not regard equality with God a thing to be grasped, but emptied Himself, taking the form of a bond-servant, and being made in the likeness of man. And being found in appearance as a man, He humbled Himself by becoming obedient to the point of death, even death on a cross."

Paul tells us five things about the proper Christian attitude:

1. Do things for the right reasons (v. 3).
2. Regard others as more important than yourself (v. 3).
3. Look out for the interests of others (v. 4).
4. Christ recognized His sonship and therefore was willing to serve God and others (v. 6).
5. Possess the attitude of Christ, who was not power hungry (v. 6),

emptied Himself (v. 7), demonstrated obedience (v. 8) and fulfilled God's purpose (v. 8).

When our emphasis of life-style is focused on verse 4, "looking out for our own personal interests," we become like the elder brother. We nurture attitudes of jealousy, pity and selfishness. Christians who possess no greater cause than themselves are not as happy as those who do not know Christ as Savior, yet have a purpose greater than themselves.

This "elder brother" attitude has three possible results, none of which are positive.

(1) It is possible for us to assume the place and privilege of a son, while refusing the obligations of a brother. The elder brother outwardly was correct, conscientious, industrious and dutiful, but look at his attitude. Also note that a wrong relationship with the brother brought a strained relationship with the father (v. 28).

(2) It is possible to serve the father faithfully, yet not be in fellowship with him. A right relationship will usually cultivate similar interest and priorities. Yet the elder brother had no idea why the father would rejoice over his son's return.

(3) It is possible to be an heir of all our Father possesses, yet have less joy and liberty than one who possesses nothing. The servants were happier than the elder son. They ate, laughed and danced, while he stood on the outside demanding his rights.

A wrong attitude kept the elder brother away from the heart's desire of the father, the love of his brother and the joy of the servants. Wrong attitudes in our lives will block the blessings of God and cause us to live below God's potential for our lives.

Attitude Application:

When our attitude begins to erode like the elder brother's, we should remember two things:

1. Our privilege: "My child, you have always been with me" (v. 31).

2. Our possessions: "All that is mine is yours" (v. 31).

Take a moment to list your privileges and possessions in Christ. How rich we are!

SECTION II
THE CONSTRUCTION
OF YOUR ATTITUDE

4

IT'S HARD TO SOAR
WITH THE EAGLES
WHEN YOU HAVE TO LIVE
WITH THE TURKEYS

"The last of the human freedoms is to choose one's attitude in any given set of circumstances."

—*Victor Frankl*

OUR SURROUNDINGS CONTROL our soaring. Turkey-thinking + turkey-talk = turkey-walk. We quickly blend into the color of our surroundings. Similarities in thinking, mannerisms, priorities, talk and opinions are very common within individual cultures. We all know married people who grow to look more alike as the years pass. Many times family members exhibit similar physical traits.

A man who had not seen his brother for many years went to the airport to pick him up. After a period of waiting one of the brothers began walking across the terminal. Without hesitation the other brother called out his name and a happy reunion followed. When asked how he recognized the other brother he replied quickly, "I knew he was my brother because he walked like my father."

It is true; we easily change to fit our environment. Our children, Elizabeth and Joel Porter, are both adopted. Although they possess their own unique identities, they also have become very similar to their adoptive parents. People who know the children are adopted continually remark about the similarities. In fact, my mother, who was recently visiting us from back east, began talking about the physical likenesses between Elizabeth and my wife Margaret. Suddenly, she exclaimed, "I

41

forgot she is adopted!"

Unquestionably our surroundings help construct our attitudes, too.

The word "choices" rises on the opposite side of the environment in the attitude construction issue. Speaking more logically than emotionally, the voice of this word says, "We are free to choose our attitudes." This logic becomes more convincing with the additional voice of Victor Frankl, survivor of a Nazi concentration camp, who said, "The last of the human freedoms is to choose one's attitude in *any* given set of circumstances." Job, ill, bereaved and poverty-stricken, refused to listen to the advice of his wife, who told him, "Curse God and die!" He rebuked her, saying, "You speak as one of the foolish women speaks. Shall we indeed accept good from God and not accept adversity?" (Job 2:10). These two viewpoints concerning how attitudes are constructed raise the question, "Which comes first, the condition or the choice?" The following chart will help us answer that question.

In our early years, our attitudes are determined mainly by our conditions. A baby does not choose his family or his environment. But as his age increases, so do his options. The difference between the two is as follows:

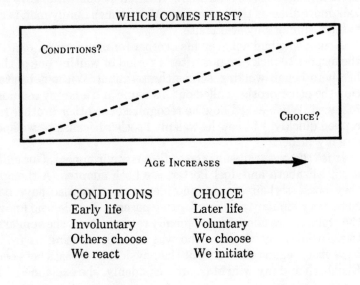

WHICH COMES FIRST?

CONDITIONS?

CHOICE?

AGE INCREASES ➜

CONDITIONS	CHOICE
Early life	Later life
Involuntary	Voluntary
Others choose	We choose
We react	We initiate

Recently I conducted a leadership seminar in Columbus, Ohio. For an entire day I talked about the importance of our attitudes and about how many times they make the difference in our lives. During one of the breaks, a man told me the following story.

"From my earliest recollections I do not remember a compliment or affirmation from my father. His father also had thought it unmanly to express affection, or even appreciation. My grandfather was a perfectionist who worked hard and expected everyone else to do the same without positive reinforcement. And since he was neither positive nor relational, he had constant turnover in employees.

"Because of my background, it has been difficult for me to encourage my family. This critical and negative attitude has hindered my work. I raised five children and lived a Christian life before them. Sadly, it is easier for them to recognize my love for God than my love for them. They are all starved for positive affirmation. The tragedy is that they have received the bad attitude trait, and now I see them passing it down to my precious grandchildren.

"Never before have I been so aware of 'catching an attitude' from surrounding conditions. Obviously, this wrong attitude has been passed along for five generations. It is now time to stop it! Today I made a conscious decision to change. This will not be done overnight, but it will be done. It will not be accomplished easily, but it will be accomplished!"

That story contains both the conditions that mold our thinking and the choice to change. Both play a vital part in the construction of our attitude. Neither can be held solely responsible for forming our mind-set.

Attitude Application:

List the conditions that have had positive and negative influences on your life (i.e., in a particular situation, you chose to find the good in the circumstance or you viewed the matter with humor).

CONDITIONS:		CHOICES:	
POSITIVE	NEGATIVE	POSITIVE	NEGATIVE

5

FOUNDATIONAL TRUTHS ABOUT THE CONSTRUCTION OF THE ATTITUDE

"The air currents of life jolt us out of line and try to keep us from achieving our goals. Unexpected weather can change our direction and strategy. We must adjust our thinking continually so we can live right."

—*John Maxwell*

BEFORE WE LOOK at specific things that help construct attitudes, we must understand some basic principles about attitude formation.

1. A child's formative years are the most important for instilling the right attitudes. Child specialists generally agree that early development in a positive setting is a main reason for the child's future successes. Attitudes we accept as children are usually the attitudes we embrace as adults. It is hard to get away from our early training. Proverbs 22:6 states, "Train up a child in the way he should go, even when he is old he will not depart from it." Why? Because the feeling and attitudes we form early in life become a part of us. We feel "comfortable" with them even though they may be wrong. Even if our attitudes make us uncomfortable, they are still difficult to change.

During my senior year of high school I decided to teach myself to play golf. For months I played incorrectly but with enthusiasm. One day on the golf course a friend told me, "John, your problem is that you are too close to the ball *after* you hit it." I had developed a slice that streaked like a banana through the sky. No problem; I just compensated for my slice. To land the ball on the fairway, I aimed for the woods on the left.

Then one day I played with an excellent golfer. The ball went

45

straight and his swing was slow. After observing a few of my boomerang shots, he offered to help. "What is wrong with my game?" I asked. "Everything!" he replied. So, the lessons began. I found out after a few weeks that it is more diffifult to learn something wrong, unlearn it and re-learn it, than to learn correctly the first time. That is certainly true about our attitudes. Those things which we feel and accept at an early age have a tendency to hang on tenaciously even when we know better and desire to change. The first impressions upon our lives are not the only impressions, but many times they are the most lasting.

2. An attitude's growth never stops. Our attitudes are formed by our experiences and how we choose to react to them. .Therefore, as long as we live, we are forming, changing or reinforcing attitudes. There is no such thing as an unalterable attitude.

We are like the little girl who was asked by her Sunday school teacher, "Who made you?" She replied, "Well, God made part of me." "What do you mean, God made part of you?" asked the surprised teacher. "Well, God made me real little, and I just growed the rest myself."

How true. The attitudes formed in our early years do not necessarily remain the same through later years. Many times marriages go through "deep waters" because of a mate's attitude change. People sometimes even switch spouses in the middle of life because of an attitude change.

My father has always been a positive influence in my life. Recently, while visiting my parents back east, I noticed he was reading Norman Vincent Peale's book, *The Power of Positive Thinking.* When I noted that he had read this book previously, he replied enthusiastically, "Of course, I must keep building my attitude."

3. The more our attitude grows on the same foundation, the more solid it becomes. Reinforcement of our foundational attitudes, whether positive or negative, makes them stronger. My father realized this truth in his commitment to read his positive-thinking books again. One of his attitude-growing practices was to write a positive thought on a 3" x 5" card and read it repeatedly throughout the day. Often I have seen him pull out

46

the card during 15-second breaks and read the positive phrase. I have decided to make this a habit of mine also. I find that the more I reinforce my mind with excellent reading the stronger I become.

4. *Many builders (specialists) help construct our attitudes at a certain time and place.* In building a home, certain specialists are needed to make the structure complete. Their time may be minimal and their contribution small, yet they are part of the construction of that home. In the same way, certain people come into our lives at various times who help make or break our perspective.

One lady wrote to me, "In my senior year of high school my English teacher took an essay that I wrote and put it on the chalkboard. She then proceeded to tear it apart in front of the class. I was humiliated and felt dumb. Then she told me that I wouldn't last one year in college. I have never forgotten that incident." One teacher, in one day, affected a self-image for an entire lifetime.

5. *There is no such thing as a perfect, flawless attitude.* In other words, we all have attitudes that need remodeling. When he taught me about airplanes, my friend Paul stated, "An aircraft hasn't been made that did not have to be trimmed." The word "trim" means to "balance in flight." Airplanes need continual adjustment in order to perform effectively. This is true of our attitudes also. The air currents of life jolt us out of line and try to keep us from achieving our goals. Unexpected weather can change our direction and strategy.

Our attitudes need adjustment with every change that comes into our lives. We need to be like the old mule owned by a Missouri farmer. One day the mule fell backward into a dry well. The farmer, fond of the animal, tried everything he could possibly think of to rescue his mule from the well. Finally, deciding rescue was impossible, he began to bury the mule. As he dumped a truckload of dirt down the well, dust began to fly and the mule began to stomp and snort. Soon old "sad face" was on top of the dirt, two feet higher than before. After a few dumped truckloads of dirt, the mule rose triumphantly to the top and walked out.

47

Everyone encounters storms and dry wells in his life which threaten to wreck his attitude. The secret to safe arrival is to continually adjust your perspective.

Attitude Application:

Our attitude does not remain stagnant. A balloon half blown up is full of air but is not filled to capacity. A rubber band pulls the object it holds together and is effective only when stretched. What are you encountering that demands the stretching of your attitude? Are you adjusting? Write a statement that identifies what you feel will be your next "storm." Now think through the strategy you'll use to counter a possible bad attitude regarding that situation.

6

MATERIALS THAT ARE USED IN CONSTRUCTING AN ATTITUDE

"People don't care how much you know until they know how much you care."

—John Maxwell

AS YOU'RE PROBABLY AWARE by this time, attitudes aren't formed automatically, and they are not shaped in a vacuum. This chapter will deal with the main influences that make our attitude what it is today. Although these "materials," listed below in chronological order, overlap, their influence is greater at some times than at others.

PERSONALITY/TEMPERAMENT
BIRTH—Environment

AGES 1-6— Word expression
Adult acceptance/affirmation

AGES 6-10— Self-image
Exposure to new experiences

AGES 11-21— Associates with peers
Physical appearance

AGES 21-61— Marriage, family, job
Assessment of your life

All these factors play an important part in our lives and cannot really be "boxed" into age zones. Yet, the diagram shows us the times they are most influential.

Attitude Application:

Take time to think through these materials that have constructed your attitudes. Write down your answers.

PERSONALITY/TEMPERAMENT: I was born into this world with a _____ personality. It affected my attitude when _____ .

ENVIRONMENT: As a child, my environment was generally (a) secure, (b) unstable, (c) intimidating.

WORD EXPRESSION: I remember a situation when someone said something positive or negative to me that affected my attitude. Explain the comment and the circumstances.

ADULT ACCEPTANCE/AFFIRMATION: From my earliest recollection I felt (a) accepted, (b) rejected by my parents.

SELF-IMAGE: Poor—Outstanding

My self-image as a child was: 1   2   3   4   5
My self-image as an adult is: 1   2   3   4   5

EXPOSURE TO NEW EXPERIENCES: One negative and one positive experience that helped cultivate my current attitude:

ASSOCIATION WITH PEERS: _____ was the first person who had a strong influence in my life. Now _____ is most important and affects my attitude the most.

PHYSICAL APPEARANCE: What do I like best about my appearance? What would I change? Why?

MARRIAGE, FAMILY, JOB: (These three areas of your life can determine your attitude to a large degree.) Which area affects me positively? Do any affect me negatively? What am I going to do about the negative influences?

SUCCESS: (Complete this sentence.) Success is _____ _____

Am I a success in the eyes of those who love me most?

ADJUSTMENTS—PHYSICAL AND EMOTIONAL: Three difficult adjustments that I have faced within the last five years:

_____

_____

_____

How has my attitude changed because of them?

ASSESSMENT OF YOUR LIFE: Up until now, my life has been (a) unfulfilled, (b) fulfilled. Life begins at_____.

Now that you've assessed how your perspective was affected in various phases of life, let's look at the specific materials that form your attitude.

Personality—Who I am

"For Thou didst form my inward parts; Thou didst weave me in my mother's womb. I will give thanks to Thee, for I am fearfully and wonderfully made; wonderful are Thy works, and my soul knows it very well" (Psalm 139:13,14).

We are born as distinct individuals. Even two children with the same parents, same environment and same training are totally different from each other. These differences contribute to the "spice of life" we all enjoy. Like tract homes that all look alike, if all people had similar personalities, our journey through life would certainly be boring.

I love the story of two men who, while fishing together, began discussing their wives. One said, "If all men were like me they would all want to be married to my wife." The other man quickly replied, "If they were all like me, none of them would want to be married to her."

A set of attitudes accompanies each personality. Generally, people with certain temperaments develop specific attitudes common to that temperament. A few years ago, pastor and counselor Tim LaHaye made us aware of four basic temperaments. Through observation, I have noticed that a person with what he calls a choleric personality often exhibits attitudes of perseverance and aggressiveness. A sanguine person will be generally positive and look on the bright side of life. The introspective melancholic can be negative at times while the phlegmatic says, "Easy come, easy go." An individual's personality is composed of a mixture of these temperaments, and there are exceptions to these examples. However, a temperament follows a track that can be identified by tracing a person's attitudes.

Environment—What's around me

"Therefore, just as through one man sin entered into the world, and death through sin, and so death spread to all men, because all sinned" (Romans 5:12).

I believe that our environment is a greater controlling factor in our attitude development than our personality or other inherited traits. Before Margaret and I began our family we decided to adopt our children. We wanted to give a child who might not normally have the benefit of a loving Christian home an opportunity to live in that environment. Although our children may not physically resemble us, they certainly have been molded by the environment in which we have reared them.

It is the environment of early childhood that develops the "belief system." The child continually picks up priorities, attitudes, interest and philosophies from his environment. It is true that *what I really believe affects my attitude!* But, what I believe may be untrue. What I believe may be unhealthy. It may hurt others and destroy me. Yet an attitude is reinforced by a belief, right or wrong.

Environment is the first influencer of our "belief system." Therefore the foundation of an attitude is laid in the environment to which we were born. Environment becomes even more significant when we realize that *the beginning attitudes are the most difficult to change!*

Because of this, when we look at society, we have a tendency to panic over the thought of bringing a child into this world. One person said, depressingly:

> *The litter is unbearable;*
> *the bottles aren't returnable;*
> *the empty cans aren't burnable;*
> *the sonic booms incredible;*
> *the tuna isn't edible;*
> *the off-shore rigs are leakable;*
> *the billboards are unspeakable;*
> *the slums are incurable;*
> *the smog is unendurable;*
> *the phosphates aren't dissolvable;*
> *the problems seem unsolvable;*

the people unforgivable; and
life has become intolerable.
—Author unknown

A Christian should not view society so negatively. With Jesus, life becomes incredible! This gives hope in every environment. The apostle Peter said that the mercy of Christ has caused us to be born to "a living hope" (1 Peter 1:3).

Still, age and Christianity do not make us immune to the influences of our environment. I pastored Faith Memorial Church in Lancaster, Ohio, for more than seven years. I remember 1978 as the year Central Ohio received many baptisms of snow and cold weather. It was then that I realized most weathermen have a bad attitude—they began giving not only the temperature but also the wind chill factor! For more than thirty days the temperature never rose above freezing. Utility bills hit an all-time high. People became claustrophobic as they were "snowed in" for days. The result: depression. I averaged 30 hours a week counseling people who battled attitude problems because of bad weather. In fact, at times I would close my eyes in prayer and listen hopefully for God to say, "Son, go to Hawaii!" Even the weather can "ice our wings" and cause us to lose altitude in our attitude.

Adult Acceptance/Affirmation—What I feel

"God demonstrates His own love toward us, in that while we were yet sinners, Christ died for us" (Romans 5:8).

Often when I am speaking to leaders, I tell them about the importance of acceptance/affirmation of the ones they are leading. The truth is, *people don't care how much you know until they know how much you care!* Think back to your school days. Who was your favorite teacher? Why? Probably your warmest memories are of someone who accepted and affirmed you. We seldom remember what our teachers said to us, but we do remember how they loved us. Long before we understand teaching we reach out for understanding. Long after we have forgotten the teachings we remember the feeling of acceptance or rejection. Many times I have asked people if they enjoyed their pastor's sermon the previous week. After a positive response I ask, "What was his subject?" Seventy-five percent of the time they cannot give me the sermon title. They do not remember the exact subject but they do remember the atmosphere and attitude in which it was delivered.

My three favorite Sunday school teachers are beautiful examples of this truth. First came Katie, my second grade teacher. When I was sick and missed her class, she would come and visit me on Monday. She would ask how I was feeling and give me a five-cent trinket that was worth a million dollars to me. Katie would say, "Johnny, I always teach better when you are in the class. When you come next Sunday morning would you raise your hand so I can see you are in attendance? Then I will teach better."

When next Sunday morning dawned I would be up, preparing to go to Sunday school. Not even the German measles, the Asian flu and the Mediterranean fruit fly combined could keep me from getting some of Katie's acceptance and affirmation! I can still remember raising my hand and watching Katie smile at me from the front of the class. I also remember other kids raising their hands when Katie began to teach, and her class grew rapidly. So, the Sunday school superintendent wanted to split the class and start a new one across the hall. He asked for volunteers for the new class and no one raised his hand. That day the second grade held the church's first sit-down strike. Our theme: "We shall not be moved." Why? No kid was about to go across the hall with a new teacher and miss Katie's continual demonstration of love.

My second favorite teacher was Roy Rogers (not Trigger's master). I had him in the fourth grade. Again, I don't remember much about what he said, but I do remember what he did. He conveyed love and acceptance to a group of fourth-grade boys by giving us his time. He took us to Ted Lewis Park and taught us to play baseball. We learned how to field grounders and make double plays. We laughed together, sweated together and got dirty together. Then, following an afternoon on the diamond, Roy would load us into his station wagon and take us to the Dairy Queen for a foot-long hot dog and a chocolate milk shake. I loved Roy Rogers!

Glen, who taught the junior boys class, was my third favorite. Did you ever teach a group of 10-wiggles-per-minute boys? Usually those teachers go straight from the class to their heavenly reward! Any teacher of this class who read about Daniel and the den of lions would say, "Big deal ... if Daniel really wanted to show his faith, they should have stuck him in a junior boys class!" Well, Glen was stuck with us. More accurately, he was stuck on us. He taught this class for twenty years. Every ornery, wiggly, unattentive boy felt Glen's love. At times, tears trickled down his face as he saw how God's love could transform junior boys.

One day Glen stopped in the middle of his lesson and said, "Boys, I pray for you every day. Right after class I need to see Steve Banner, Phil Conrad, Junior Fowler and John Maxwell." After class, the four of us huddled in the corner with Glen, and he said, "Last night while I was praying for you, I sensed that the Lord was going to call each of you into full-time Christian service. I want to be the first to encourage you to obey God." Then he wept as he prayed, asking the Lord to use us for His glory. Today we all pastor churches—Steve Banner in Ohio, Phil Conrad in Arizona, Junior Fowler in Oklahoma and I in California. These Sunday school teachers made a positive mark on my life because of their acceptance and affirmation.

Recently I talked with Mary Vaughn, who was once the head of counseling in the Cincinnati elementary school system. I asked her to pinpoint the main problem she noticed in counseling situations. "John," she said immediately, "most children's psychological problems stem from their lack of acceptance and affirmation from parents and peers." Mary continually emphasized that economic level, professional or social strata and other factors in which society puts so much value were insignificant.

Then she told me a story about Dennis, aged 10. This third-grader was always fighting, lying, and causing disturbances with his classmates. He believed "no one likes me, the teacher just picks on me." He would not respond to the people who really cared for him and tried to help the most. His problem? He wanted his mother's affirmation and love so much that he lived in a fantasy world, always talking of his mother's love. In reality, his mother did nothing to affirm him. Dennis' need for care was so great that he fantasized about his mother's love and directed his bad attitude toward others.

Unlike Dennis, I was privileged to grow up in a very affirming family. I never questioned my parents' love and acceptance. They were continually affirming their love through action and words. Now, Margaret and I have tried to create this same environment for our children. The other day we were talking about the importance of showing love to our children. We concluded that our kids see or sense our acceptance and affirmation at least thirty times a day. That's not too much! Have you ever been told too many times that you are important, loved and appreciated? Remember, *people don't care how much you know until they know how much you care.*

Word Expressions—What I Hear

"Faith comes from hearing . . . " (Romans 5:17).

> "Sticks and stones may break my bones
> but names will never hurt me."

Don't you believe that! In fact, after the bruises have disappeared, and the physical pain is gone, the inward pain of hurtful words remains. During one of our staff meetings I asked the pastors, secretaries and custodians to raise their hands if they could remember a childhood experience that hurt deeply because of someone's words. Everyone raised his hand. One pastor recalled the time when he sat in a reading circle at school. (Do you remember how intimidating those sessions were?) When his time came to read, he mispronounced the word "photography." He read it *photo-graphy* instead of *photog'-ra-phy*. The teacher corrected him and the class laughed. He still remembers . . . forty years later. One positive result of that experience was Chuck's desire from that moment on to pronounce words correctly. Today he excels as a speaker because of that determination.

Another pastor on my staff told the group about his beginning days at seminary. He felt overwhelmed and intimidated by his new experience. The work load seemed impossible. There were thousands of pages to read, Greek words to learn, Scripture verses to memorize and papers to write. Although he hadn't told anyone about the pressure he was feeling, it was obvious to those around him. Noticing his distress, an upper classman walked up, put his arm around his shoulder and said, "Friend, I want to share something with you. It doesn't matter how big the rock is. If you just keep pounding, it's gonna bust." The pastor said, "Suddenly, my huge rock became manageable and I started pounding steadily, little by little. And sure enough, right on schedule (three years later) the rock 'busted' and they called it graduation." That time, words brought encouragement instead of hurt.

Words are powerful ... yet meaningless until they are attached to a context. The same words coming from two different people are very seldom received in the same way. The same words phrased differently seldom have the same impact. The same words coming from the same person will usually be interpreted in light of the speaker's attitude. One father tried to teach his son this truth. One day the boy came home and said, "Dad, I think I flunked my arithmetic test." His dad said, "Son, don't say that; that's negative. Be positive." So the boy said, "Dad, I am positive I flunked my arithmetic test."

Words can encourage either the stretching or shrinking of our lives. If most of our conversations contain a negative bent, I am convinced it is better to say nothing. Years ago new engineers in General Electric's lamp division were assigned, as a joke, the impossible task of frosting bulbs on the inside. Eventually, however, an undaunted newcomer named Marvin Papkin not only found a way to frost bulbs on the inside, but also developed an etching acid which left minutely rounded pits on the surface instead of sharp depressions. This strengthened each bulb. No one had told him it *couldn't* be done, so he did it!

Self-image—How I see myself

"For as he thinks within himself, so he is" (Proverbs 23:7).

It is impossible to perform consistently in a manner inconsistent with the way we see ourselves. In other words, we usually act in direct response to our self-image. Nothing is more difficult to accomplish than changing outward actions without changing inward feelings. As we realize our performance is based on our perception of ourselves, we should also remember God's unconditional love and acceptance. He thinks more of us than we do ourselves. The disciples may not have been high achievers in the sight of the world, but the call of Christ turned their lives around.

One of the best ways to improve those inward feelings is to

put some "success" under your belt. My daughter Elizabeth just turned seven and is in the first grade. She had a tendency to be shy and wants to hold back on new experiences. But once she has "warmed up" to a situation, it's "full steam ahead." Recently her school had a candy bar sale to help lift its financial burden. Each child was given thirty candy bars and was challenged to sell every one of them. When I picked up Elizabeth from school she was holding her "challenge" and needed some positive encouragement. It was time for a "sales" meeting with my new salesgirl.

All the way home I taught her how to sell candy bars. I surrounded each teaching point with a half dozen "You can do it—your smile will win them over—I believe in you" phrases. By the end of our fifteen-minute drive, the young lady sitting beside me had become a charming, committed saleslady. Off she went to the neighborhood with little brother Joel eating one of the candy bars and declaring that it was truly the best he had ever devoured. At the end of the day, all thirty bars had been sold and Elizabeth was feeling great. I will never forget the words she prayed as I tucked her into bed that night: "O God, thanks for the candy sale at school. It's great. O Lord, help make me a winner! Amen."

This prayer is the heart's desire of every person. We want to be winners. Sure enough, Elizabeth came home the next day with another box of candy bars. Now the big test! She'd exhausted the supply of friendly neighbors, and she was thrust out into the cruel world of the unknown buyer. Elizabeth admitted fear as we went to a shopping center to sell our wares. Again, I offered more encouragement, a few more selling tips, more encouragement, the right location, *more* encouragement. She did it. The experience amounted to two days of selling, two sold-out performances, two happy people and one boosted self-image.

I like the self-esteem demonstrated by the little fellow who excitedly pulled a cornstalk out by its roots. When his father congratulated him, he beamed, "And just think," he said, "the whole world had hold of the other end of it!"

Compare him with Shauna, a sixth grader. She usually behaved like a smark aleck and remained cocky, even when she had been caught stealing. When confronted about the theft, she said she did it to get revenge on her parents. She was not remorseful. Counseling sessions revealed that Shauna rarely saw her father, and he did not love her. When they were together, she seldom received acceptance or a feeling of importance. She saw herself as she thought her father saw her. Shauna's counselor continually gave her sincere compliments and modeled to the parents the necessary ingredients for creating a proper self-image. In time, Shauna's sense of self worth improved.

The principle works in reverse too. How we see ourselves reflects how others see us. If we like ourselves it increases the odds that others will like us also. *Self-image is the parameter to the construction of our attitude.* We act in response to how we see ourselves. We will never go beyond the boundaries that stake out our true feelings about ourselves. Those "other countries" can be explored only when our self-image is strong enough to give permission.

Exposure to New Experiences—Opportunities for growth

Paul said, "Brethren, I do not regard myself as having laid hold of it yet; but one thing I do: forgetting what lies behind and reaching forward to what lies ahead, I press on toward the goal for the prize of the upward call of God in Christ Jesus" (Philippians 3:13-14).

Voltaire likened life to a game of cards. Each player must accept the cards dealt to him. But once those cards are in the hand, he or she alone decides how to play them to win the game.

We always have a number of opportunities in our hand. We must decide whether to take a risk and act on them. Nothing in life causes more stress, yet at the same time provides more opportunity for growth, than new experiences. The familiar poem,

> *"My life may touch a dozen lives*
> *Before this day is done;*
> *Leave countless marks for good or ill*
> *E'er sets the evening sun."*

speaks of the power of influence.

That first line, with one word changed, can illustrate the effect of new experiences on a life.

> My life may *experience* a dozen lives
> Before this day is done;
> Leave countless marks for good or ill
> E'er sets the evening sun

My parents recognized the value of new experiences and did their best to expose each child to positive ones. Some of my fondest memories are of times when I traveled with my father. Many times he would say to my teacher, "You are doing an excellent job teaching my son, but for the next week I am going to take him with me and open up some new experiences for him." Off we would go to another state, and my awareness of people, nature and culture would be heightened.

I will always be especially grateful for those pre-arranged new experiences. I'll never forget the time I met the great missionary statesman, E. Stanley Jones. After listening to this spiritual giant speak, my father took me into a side office to meet him! I can still remember the room, his attitude and, most important, his words of encouragement to me.

As a parent, it is impossible for you to shield your children from the "cards," the new experiences that might be negative. Also, it is essential to prepare positive encounters that will build self-image and confidence. Both positive and negative experiences should be used as tools in preparing children for life.

Elizabeth's story didn't end after two successful selling days. Later she went door-to-door again, encouraging people to buy the "world's most delicious chocolate bar." I followed her in the car. Repeatedly she smiled, told her story and had no luck. Repeatedly I smiled and encouraged her not to quit. I was careful to stress that winning is trying. We set a goal (the end of a very long block) and determined not to quit until that goal was reached. With each "no sale" visit her steps became slower and my enthusiasm greater. Finally, she made a sale at the next to the last house. She came running back to the car, waving money and wanting to go one more block. I said, "fine" and off she ran.

The lesson is obvious. Children need continual reassurance and praise when their new experiences are less than positive. In fact, the worse the experience, the more encouragement they need. But sometimes we become discouraged when they are discouraged. This is a good formula to adopt:

New experiences + teaching applications × love = growth.

Association With Peers—Who influences me

"A man of many friends comes to ruin, but there is a friend who sticks closer than a brother" (Proverbs 18:24).

What others indicate about their perceptions of us affects how we perceive ourselves. Usually we respond to the expectations of others. This truth becomes evident to the parent when his child goes to school. No longer can the parent control his child's environment. Any elementary teacher understands that kids very quickly develop a "pecking order" for the class. Students acquire labels and children relate to each other with sometimes cruel honesty. Peer pressure becomes a problem.

Mary Vaughn, in one of her case studies involving a first grader, wrote: "A very poor environment physically (little clothing, shelter, or food) does not necessarily produce negative attitudes in the child. It is the lack of acceptance by peers that form scars deep within the child." Her example: A first grader who was stealing.

Terry looked pale and sickly. The teacher was concerned about his stealing. Missing things were usually found in his desk. After counseling with Terry, a home visit was arranged with his parents. Their dwelling contained four rooms and housed nine people. The rooms were scarcely furnished and poverty was evident. The parents were grateful for the offer of assistance and clothing. They were also willing to help Terry. Assessment of problem: Terry stole only because peer pressure made him aware of his poverty. He wanted the same cute erasers and lunch boxes his friends had.

No doubt this experience helped Terry's parents realize that others exercised a sizable amount of control over their son's behavior. My parents understood this fact also and determined to watch and control our peer relationships as much as possible.

Their strategy: Provide a climate in the Maxwell home that was appealing to their two boys' friends. This meant sacrificing their finances and time. They provided us with a shuffleboard game, ping pong table, pool table, pin ball machine, chemistry set, basketball court and all the sports equipment that had been invented. We also had one mother who was spectator, referee, counselor, arbitrator and fan.

And the kids came, often 20 to 25 at a time. All sizes, shapes and colors. Everyone had fun and my parents observed our friends. Sometimes, after the gang had gone, my parents would ask about one of our friends. They would openly discuss his language or attitudes and encourage us to not act or think that way. I realize now that most of my major decisions as a young boy were influenced by my parents' teaching and observation of my associations.

My folks didn't limit their observations to my youth. When my father realized that Margaret and I were dating steadily, he spent a day driving to her home town and talking with her parents, pastor and school teachers to better understand the kind of girl his son was dating. Although he never told me this story until we were married, I know the reports he received were very favorable. He encouraged me to marry her! Now, I wouldn't recommend such close observation to every parent, but his interest demonstrated love to me.

Casey Stengel, a successful manager of the New York Yankees baseball team, understood the power of associations on a ball player's attitude. Billy Martin remembers Stengel's advice to him when Martin was a rookie manager. "Casey said there would be fifteen players on your team who will run through a wall for you, five who will hate you and five who are undecided," Martin said. Stengel added. "When you make out your rooming list, always room your losers together. Never room a good guy with a loser. Those losers who stay together will blame the manager for everything but it won't spread if you keep them isolated."

Recently a man came up to me after I had spoken about attitudes and associates. He wanted me to clarify the concept of isolating ourselves from others who can "drag us down." His question was, "How can we help others who have attitude problems if we stay away from them?" My answer: "There is a difference between helping those with perpetual attitude problems and enlisting them as our close friends. The closer our relationship, the more influential the attitudes and philosophies of our friends become to us." Charles "Tremendous"

Jones, author of *Life is Tremendous,* said, "What you will become in five years will be determined by what you read and who you associate with." That's good advice for us all.

Physical Appearance—How we look to others

" ... man looks at the outward appearance, but the Lord looks at the heart" (1 Samuel 16:7).

Our looks play an important part in the construction of our attitude. Incredible pressure is placed upon people to possess that "in look" which is the standard of acceptance. For one day, while you're watching television, notice how the commercials emphasize looks. Notice the percentage of ads dealing with clothing, diet, exercise and overall physical attractiveness. Hollywood says "homeliness is out and handsomeness is in." This influences our perceptions of our worth, based on physical appearance. What can make it even more difficult is the realization that others judge our worth also by our appearance. Recently I read a business article which stated, "Our physical attractiveness helps determine our income." The research reported in that article showed the discrepancies between the salaries of men 6'2" and 5'10". The taller men consistently received higher salaries.

Marriage, Family and Job—Our security and status

"God is our refuge and strength, a very present help in trouble" (Psalm 46:1).

New influences begin to affect our attitude as we approach our middle twenties. It is during this time of our lives that most of us marry. That means another person influences our perspective.

When I speak on attitudes, I always emphasize the need to surround ourselves with positive people. One of the saddest comments that I often receive comes from one mate who tells me that the other marriage partner is negative and doesn't want to change. To a certain extent, when the negative mate does not want to change, the positive one is imprisoned by negativism. In such situations, I advise the couple to remember and return to patterns they followed in their courtship days.

Observe a couple during courtship. They are illustrating two beautiful ideas. They are building on strengths and expecting the best.

This is when the girl tends to see the guy as a knight in shining armor. She's been looking for his best. She's been expecting his best. She ignores anything that seems to be a weakness. The man sees a beautiful girl with noble feelings and fine qualities. Then they get married, and each one sees the reality of the other—both strengths and weaknesses. The marriage will be good and reinforcing if the weaknesses are not emphasized. By many end up in divorce court because the strengths are ignored! The partners go from expecting the best to expecting the worst, from building on strengths to focusing on weaknesses.

Whether you are 11, 42, or 65, your attitude toward life is still under construction. By understanding the materials that are part of your attitude structures, you and those you influence can maintain a healthier perspective.

7

THE COSTLIEST MISTAKE THAT PEOPLE MAKE IN CONSTRUCTING AN ATTITUDE

"Many intelligent adults ... are restrained in thoughts, actions and results. They never move further than the boundaries of their self-imposed limitation."

—John Maxwell

IT HAPPENS TO US the moment we are born. Excited family members press their noses against the nursery window in the hospital and begin playing the game, "Who does he look like?" After much discussion, it is decided that the red-faced, wrinkly, toothless, bald baby looks like "Uncle Harry." The labeling of the little child increases as his personality develops. That is a normal human reaction. We all do it. It becomes hurtful, however, when we start placing limitations on our child because he is a *"C"*student, a "fair" runner or a "plain" child. Unless parents exercise care, their children will grow up selling themselves short because of the "box" parents put them in, the expectations parents have placed upon them.

One "boxed in" child was Adam Clarke, who was born in the eighteenth century in Ireland. When Adam was a schoolboy, his father told the teacher that Adam wouldn't do well.

The teacher said, "He looks bright."

That statement changed his life—let him out of the box his father had put him in. He lived to be 72, and he became a great scholar, an English Methodist preacher, and an author of commentaries and a book called *Christian Theology*. When Adam Clarke preached, it was said, people listened. (From *When Adam Clarke Preached, People Listened*, by Wesley Tracy, Kansas City, Missouri: Beacon Hill Press, n.d., pp. 13, 14.)

What are a person's capabilities? No one knows. Therefore, no one should be consciously instilling life-limiting thoughts into others. Thirty years ago, Johnny Weissmuller, also known as Tarzan to movie viewers, was called the greatest swimmer the world had ever known. Doctors and coaches around the world said, "Nobody will ever break Johnny Weissmuller's records." He held more than fifty of them! Do you know who is breaking Tarzan's records today? Thirteen-year-old girls! The 1936 Olympic records were the *qualifying* standards for the 1972 Olympics.

For decades, track enthusiasts declared boldly that nobody would break the four-minute mile. For decades their prediction looked secure. Roger Bannister did not listen to such limiting assumptions. Result: he broke the "impossible" four-minute mile. Today, at least 336 men have accomplished this feat. They did not let themselves be limited by others' expectations.

Remember: Others can stop you temporarily, but you are the only one who can do it permanently.

An elephant can easily pick up a one-ton load with his trunk. But have you ever visited a circus and watched these huge creatures standing quietly tied to a small wooden stake?

While still young and weak, an elephant is tied by a heavy chain to an immovable iron stake. He discovers that, no matter how hard he tries, he cannot break the chain or move the stake. Then, no matter how large and strong the elephant becomes, he continues to believe he cannot move as long as he can see the stake in the ground beside him.

Many intelligent adults behave like the circus elephant. They are restrained in thought, action and results. They never move further than the boundaries of self-imposed limitation.

Often when lecturing on limitations, I talk about what I call the "sap strata."

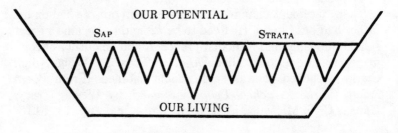

In this illustration, the sap strata line represents our self-imposed, limiting barrier. The jagged line that keeps rising and falling pictures our actual living. The effort it would take to break through that sap strata level takes the "sap" out of us. Every time we make an attempt to break through the line, there is an accompanying pain. We pay a physical and emotional price when we actually break through our perceived limitations and enter into a new area of further potential.

Later, in Sections III and IV of this book, we will take a closer look at this process. Sadly, many people accept their sap strata and never reach their potential. They are like the trained fleas that jump up and down in a canister. The observant bystander will notice that the jar has no lid to keep the fleas inside. So, why don't those fleas jump out of the container to their freedom? The answer is simple. The flea trainer, when first placing the fleas into the canister also puts the lid on top. The fleas jump high and continually bash their little flea brains on the lid. After a few "Excedrin headaches" the fleas quit jumping quite so high and enjoy their new-found comfort. Now the lid can be removed and the fleas are held captive; not by a real lid, but by a mind-set that says, "so high and no more."

Mark Twain once said, "If a cat sits on a hot stove, that cat will never sit on a *hot* stove again." He continued, "That cat will never sit on a *cold* stove, either." Conclusion: That cat will associate stoves with a bad, hot experience and say, "Never again." We all encounter bad experiences and no one likes to take the "medicine." Yet we penalize ourselves and others when we put "lids" on potential.

I've listed below a few comments we unthinkingly make that can limit potential and keep us from breaking through the sap strata.

"It's never been done before."
"I'll never try that again."
"Take it easy."

Now it's your turn. Make a list of statements that have limited your potential:

If someone tries to saddle you with a sap strata, here's a poem that can counter the attack. Read it from time to time.

67

IT COULDN'T BE DONE

Somebody said that it couldn't be done,
But he with a chuckle replied
That maybe it couldn't, but he would be one
Who wouldn't say so 'till he tried.
So he buckled right in with the trace of a grin
On his face. If he worried, he hid it.
He started to sing as he tackled the thing
That couldn't be done, and he did it.

Somebody scoffed: "Oh, you'll never do that;
At least no one ever has done it;"
But he took off his coat and took off his hat
And the first thing he knew he'd begun it.
With the lift of his chin and a bit of a grin,
Without any doubting or quiddit,
He started to sing as he tackled the thing
That couldn't be done, and he did it.

There are thousands to tell you it cannot be done,
There are thousands to prophesy failure;
There are thousands to point out to you, one by one,
The dangers that wait to assail you.
But just buckle right in with a bit of a grin,
Then take off your coat and go to it;
Just start in to sing as you tackle the thing
That "cannot be done," and you'll do it.

—Edgar A. Guest

SECTION III
THE CRASHING OF YOUR ATTITUDE

8

Mayday! Mayday! My Attitude is Losing Altitude

Therefore, since we have so great a cloud of witnesses surrounding us, let us lay aside every encumbrance, and the sin which so easily entangles us, and let us run with endurance the race that is set before us, fixing our eyes on Jesus (Hebrews 12:1,2).

ONE OF THE FIRST THINGS I discovered during my ride in a small airplane was that turbulence often makes the ride a little rough. Just as flying has its "rough" weather, so does life. A smooth day is the exception, not the norm. Flying straight and level usually comes as a *recovery* from climbs, descents and turns. It is the exception, not the rule.

Have you ever had a day like the small boy had in *Alexander and the Terrible, Horrible, No Good, Very Bad Day*, by Judith Viorst?

"I went to sleep with gum in my mouth and now there's gum in my hair and when I got out of bed this morning I tripped on the skateboard and by mistake I dropped my sweater in the sink while the water was running and I could tell it was going to be a terrible, horrible, no good, very bad day.

"At breakfast Anthony found a Corvette Sting Ray car kit in his breakfast cereal box and Nick found a Junior Undercover Agent code ring in his breakfast cereal box, but in my breakfast cereal box all I found was breakfast cereal.

"I think I'll move to Australia.

"In the car pool Mrs. Gibson let Becky have a seat by the window. Audrey and Elliot got seats by the window too. I said I was being scrunched, I said I was being smushed. I said, 'If I don't get a seat by the window I am going to be car-sick.' No one even answered.

"I could tell it was going to be a terrible, horrible, no good, very bad day.

"At school Mrs. Dickens liked Paul's picture of the sailboat better than my picture of the invisible castle.

"At singing time she said I sang too loud. At counting time she said I left out sixteen. Who needs sixteen? I could tell it was going to be a terrible, horrible, no good, very bad day.

"I could tell because Paul said I wasn't his best friend anymore. He said that Philip Parker was his best friend, and that Albert Moyo was his next best friend and that I was only his third best friend.

"'I hope you sit on a tack,' I said to Paul. 'I hope the next time you get a double-decker strawberry ice cream cone the ice cream part falls off the cone part and lands in Australia.'

"There were two cupcakes in Philip Parker's lunch bag and Albert got a Hershey bar with almonds and Paul's mother gave him a piece of jelly roll that had little coconut sprinkles on the top. Guess whose mother forgot to put in dessert?

"It was a terrible, horrible, no good, very bad day.

"That's what it was because after school my mom took us all to the dentist and Dr. Fields found a cavity just in me. 'Come back next week and I'll fix it,' said Dr. Fields. 'Next week,' I said, 'I'm going to Australia.'

"On the way downstairs the elevator door closed on my foot and while we were waiting for my mom to go get the car, Anthony made me fall where it was muddy and when I started crying because of the mud, Nick said I was a crybaby and while I was punching Nick for saying crybaby my mom came back with the car and scolded me for being muddy and fighting.

"'I am having a terrible, horrible, no good, very bad day,' I told everybody. No one even answered.

"So then we went to the shoe store to buy some sneakers. Anthony chose white ones with blue stripes. Nick chose red ones with white stripes. I chose blue ones with red stripes, but then the shoe man said 'We're all sold out.' They made me buy plain old white ones, but they can't make me wear them.

"When we picked up my dad at his office he said I couldn't play with his copying machine, but I forgot. He also said to watch out for the books on his desk, and I was careful as could be except for my elbow. He also said 'don't fool around with the phone,' but I think I called Australia. My dad said please don't pick him up anymore. It was a terrible, horrible, no good, very bad day.

"There were lima beans for dinner and I hate limas. There was kissing on TV and I hate kissing.

"My bath was too hot, I got soap in my eyes, my marble went down the drain, and I had to wear my railroad pajamas. I hate my railroad pajamas.

"When I went to bed Nick took back the pillow he said I could keep and the Mickey Mouse night light burned out and I bit my tongue. The cat wants to sleep with Anthony, not with me.

"It has been a terrible, horrible, no good, very bad day. My mom says some days are like that. Even in Australia." (Published by Atheneum Publishers, New York, 1976.)

Here are some rules to remember when you have one of those terrible, horrible, no good, very bad days and your attitude starts to plummet:

RULE 1: *Maintain the right attitude when the "going gets tough."*

Our natural reaction is to bail out of the right attitude to compensate for our problems. During our flight of life our attitude is most critical during the "tough times." That is when we are tempted to panic and make bad attitude decisions. When we crash, it comes from a wrong reaction, not the turbulence. How often have we seen the "making a mountain out of a molehill" response become more dangerous than the problem itself?

Remember, the difficulty really becomes a problem when we internalize unfortunate circumstances. Another thing to remember when the weather gets rough, is that *what really matters is what happens in us, not to us!* When the external circumstances lead to wrong internal reactions, we really have problems. Recently I talked to a man who was having financial difficulty. He faced the prospect of losing everything. I offered prayer and encouragement during this difficult time. His reaction: "I've never been closer to God!" He told how this trial was making him stronger in his walk with God. Paul told Timothy that the Christians would be persecuted. He also said that not only had he endured persecution, but also that God had always delivered him (2 Timothy 3:11,12). Paul allowed the storms of life to strengthen him. How different from those who yell "I quit" every time difficulty arises.

James even tells us that those problems are good. "Consider it all joy, my brethren, when you encounter various trials [why?], knowing that the testing of your faith produces endurance. And let endurance have its perfect result, that you may be perfect and complete, lacking in nothing" (James 1:2-4).

RULE 2: *Realize that the "rough weather" will not last forever.*

When you're caught in the middle of touchy situations it is often difficult to remember this trust. We become consumed with the problems. Our entire outlook is colored by the present. A drowning man is not concerned about tomorrow's schedule.

There is an expression I use quite often when I sense that the difficulties of the day are overwhelming me. At the moment when I have "had enough" I say, "This too shall pass!" That brief statement really works. It helps me gain perspective on my situation.

Still, "rough weather" wears us down. Many times it is not the size of the problem, but the length of it that weighs heavily on us. That is why Paul teaches the church at Galatia, "let us not lose heart in doing good, for in due time we shall reap if we do not grow weary" (6:9). Many times preachers will say, "What we sow we reap." Paul says that it is possible to sow and not reap the benefits. How? By not holding steady and being patient enough to wait.

Many times I have heard runners talk about the "highs" they receive in running. (It is hard to convince me of their claim when I observe the grimaces on their faces as they run.) Once they receive their "second wind," they feel like they could run all day. Their secret? Run until you get your second wind. The first part is difficult and painful. The last part is easier and fruitful.

"Therefore, since we have so great a cloud of witnesses surrounding us, let us lay aside every encumbrance, and the sin which so easily entangles us, and let us run with endurance the race that is set before us, fixing our eyes on Jesus, the author and perfecter of faith, who for the joy set before Him endured the cross, despising the shame, and has sat down at the right hand of the throne of God. For consider Him who has endured such hostility by sinners against Himself, so that you may not grow weary and lose heart" (Hebrews 12:1-3).

RULE 3: *Try to make major decisions before the storm.*

Many storms can be avoided by thinking and planning ahead. A pilot will check the weather in his planned flight area before he makes his decision to proceed. When flying, he will check his radar or call ahead to anticipate weather conditions.

Obviously, not all storms can be avoided. Yet, I wonder how many we encounter because we fail to check all the resources available to us. Too many times our troubles are a result of our own poor planning and not the conditions that surround our lives.

One of my college professors became a campus conversation piece because of his horrible driving. Kids would say things like, "I left class early so I could get home safely before Professor Gladstone got on the road." After the professor had three accidents in six weeks, a student said to his wife sympathetically, "The devil sure has been causing your husband problems in his driving." Her reply, "Honey, don't blame the devil, George never could drive."

To avoid some potential storms in life we need to know and rely on rough weather indicators. I've listed some possible "eyes" that can help us foresee trouble, and questions we should ask before proceeding toward solving the problem:

ROUGH WEATHER INDICATORS	QUESTIONS TO ASK MYSELF
Lack of experience	Do I know someone with *successful* experience in this area?
Lack of knowledge	Have I studied sufficiently to direct my course effectively?
Lack of time	Did I allow the process of time to work on me as well as the storm?
Lack of facts	Are all the facts gathered to allow a proper decision?

Lack of prayer	Is this idea God's or mine? If mine, does God bless it and back it through the Word?

Even after all the weather indicators have been checked, we will still probably encounter some storms. Life's difficulties have a crazy way of sneaking up on us. When that happens, try to delay as many major decisions as possible. Our life is a series of "ups and downs." (See illustration.) There is one major difference between people who jump from one major problem to another and those who go from one major success to the next. The difference is timing.

Those who make one bad decision after another make their major decisions during the "lows" of life. Those who exhibit the "Midas touch" have learned to wait until the "lows" pass and they feel on top of things.

When do you make the big "D"?

The right time to make a decision

The wrong time to make decision

I cringe when I hear seminar speakers say, "It is more important to make the wrong decision immediately than no decision." Don't you believe it! The key to success in decision making is as much timing as making the right choice.

The wrong decision at the wrong time = disaster.
The wrong decision at the right time = mistake.
The right decision at the wrong time = unacceptance.
The right decision at the right time = success.

Usually wrong decisions are made at the wrong time and right decisions are made at the right time. The reason? We let our environment control our thinking, which controls our decisions. Therefore, the more decisions that are made in the calm of life, the fewer times storms can bring us down. God can use the fruit of our bad decisions for good, but we can avoid compounding our problems by making decisions at the best time.

RULE 4: *Keep in contact with the control tower.*

Every pilot knows the value of communicating with knowledgeable men during times of trouble. The natural reaction when having difficulty in the sky is to radio for help. We do not always do this in our daily living.

Our tendency is often to "try to make it on our own." We admire that rugged, independent individual who "pulled himself up by his bootstraps." That is the American way. At times we are all little Frank Sinatras belting out for all to hear, "I did it my way."

Jesus sings another song. Its words speak about fullness of joy and fruitfulness. The thesis of His song states, "Apart from Me you can do nothing" (John 15:5). The title of His song is "Abide in Me and I in You" or more modernly stated, "You'll Be Fine If You're Connected to the Vine."

Stanza 1 says, "Abide in Me, and I in you. As the branch cannot bear fruit of itself, unless it abides in the vine, so neither can you unless you abide in Me" (John 15:4).

Stanza 2 says, "I am the Vine, you are the branches; he who abides in Me, and I in him, he bears much fruit; for apart from Me you can do nothing" (John 15:5).

Stanza 3 says, "If anyone does not abide in Me, he is thrown away as a branch, and dries up; and they gather them and cast them into the fire, and they are burned" (John 15:6).

Stanza 4 says, "If you abide in Me, and My words abide in you, ask whatever you wish, and it shall be done for you" (John 15:7).

Recently, during a time of revival at my church, God began dealing with me about Jesus' statements, "Apart from Me you can do nothing." I have always been prone to think, "Apart from God, I can only do some things." I would admit quickly my need for Him to do "exceeding abundantly beyond all that we ask or think ... ," but that which was less than extraordinary I felt sufficient to accomplish by myself. I learned that I can fly solo in my world no longer. Whether I'm in rough weather or in calm, blue skies, I must keep in contact with Christ.

Attitude Application:

I've made the following statements in this chapter. Take a moment and apply these truths to your present attitude.

1. "What really matters is what happens in us, not to us."
   Which is more important—wrong action directed at me or wrong reaction within me?
   Why?

2. "What we sow, we always reap." Is that true?
   If not, why?

3. "The difference between success and failure in decision making is often timing."
   When does a winner make his decisions?
   When do I make mine?

4. "We admire that rugged, independent individual who 'pulled himself up by his bootstraps' and made it on his own. That is the American way."
   What is God's way? Read 2 Corinthians 1:18-31; 2:1-5.

We talked about factors that cause us to lose altitude. The following chapters of Section III are "crash causers." These are either the things that cause us to crash, or the things we blame when we make uncomfortable landings.

9

THE CRASH FROM WITHIN

"There is no security on this earth. There is only opportunity."
—Douglas MacArthur

THERE ARE CERTAIN STORMS within a person's life that contribute to an altitude crash. The three storms I'm discussing in this chapter are predominantly inward, not outward. They are part of us and must be constructively dealt with to bring inner peace and a wholesome attitude.

The first inward storm is: *The Fear of Failure.*

We have many ways of dealing with it. Some people determine, "If at first you don't succeed, destroy all the evidence that you've tried."

> Failure—We hide it
> deny it
> fear it
> ignore it and
> hate it

We do everything but accept it. By acceptance, I don't mean resignation and apathy. I mean understanding that failure is a necessary step to success. The man who never made a mistake never did anything!

I enjoy reading about the lives of great men. One consistent fact I notice is all successful people experienced failure. In fact, most of them began as failures.

When the great Polish pianist, Ignace Paderewski, first chose to study the piano, his music teacher told him his hands were much too small to master the keyboard.

When the great Italian tenor, Enrico Caruso, first applied for instruction, the teacher told him his voice sounded like the wind whistling through the window.

When the great statesman of Victorian England, Benjamin Disraeli, attempted to speak in Parliament for the first time, members hissed him into silence and laughed when he said, "Though I sit down now, the time will come when you will hear of me."

Henry Ford forgot to put a reverse gear in his first car.

Thomas Edison spent $2,000,000 on an invention which proved to be of little value.

Very little comes out right the first time. Failures, repeated failures, are fingerprints on the road to achievement. Abraham Lincoln's life could demonstrate that the only time you don't fail is the last time you try something and it works. We can "fail forward" toward success.

ABRAHAM LINCOLN—Biography of a Failure:

> Difficult childhood
> Less than one year formal schooling
> Failed in business in 1831
> Defeated for legislature, '32
> Again failed in business, '33
> Elected to legislature, '34
> Fiancee died, '35
> Defeated for Speaker, '38
> Defeated for Elector, '40
> Married, wife a burden, '42
> Only one of his four sons lived past age 18
> Defeated for Congress, '43
> Elected to Congress, '46
> Defeated for Congress, '48
> Defeated for Senate, '55
> Defeated for Vice-President, '56
> Defeated for Senate, '58
> Elected President, '60

Accepting failure in the positive sense becomes effective when you believe that the right to fail is as important as the right to succeed. I enjoy the weather in San Diego more than the Southern California natives. Why? Because I lived in Ohio and experienced the winter of '78, not to mention a few others.

Most people seldom value their good health until they become ill. Exposure to the problems gives greater joy in our progress if we can accept failure as an important process in reaching our goal.

It is impossible to succeed without suffering. If you are successful and have not suffered, someone has suffered for you; and if you are suffering without succeeding, perhaps someone may succeed after you. But there is no success without suffering.

A few years ago while speaking in Dallas, I took a poll among church leaders, asking this question: "What keeps you from building a great work for God?" The number one answer: "Fear of failure." Immediately I began speaking to leaders about failure. My closing message at a large conference where pastors had seen and heard success stories was on "Flops, Failures and Fumbles." The total content of that 45-minute address consisted of all my programs that had fizzled. The crowd laughed hysterically as I openly confessed my many mistakes. Then they hurriedly bought a copy of the message. Why? I had just admitted failure and given them permission to do the same.

This year I listened to Reuben Welch, author of *We Really Do Need Each Other,* speak the same liberating truth. He talked about how, when we're merely concerned about survival and maintaining the status quo, we strive for a reputation that stifles progress and becomes self-limiting. After hearing that message I had a plaque made that said, "I don't have to survive."

Our Lord not only taught this truth, but He also demonstrated it. He said that dying, not living, was the key to effectiveness. "Truly, truly, I say to you, unless a grain of wheat falls into the earth and dies, it remains by itself alone; but if it dies, it bears much fruit. He who loves his life loses it; and he who hates his life in this world shall keep it to life eternal" (John 12:24,25).

A few chapters later we read how Christ demonstrated this truth at Calvary. He became a visual example of His words, "Greater love has no one than this, that one lay down his life for his friends" (John 15:13). Certainly the "survival syndrome" was not a part of Jesus' life.

The apostle Paul understood this teaching by saying of himself, "I have been crucified with Christ; and it is no longer I who live, but Christ lives in me; and the life which I now live in the flesh, I live by faith in the Son of God, who loved me, and delivered Himself up for me" (Galatians 2:20).

Tertullian, a second-century apologist, addressed this survival issue early in the history of the church. Some of the Christians were making idols as their profession. When faced with the issue of Christians working in the idol-making business, their reply was, "We must live." Tertullian retorted with the question, "Must you live?" His point: It is more important to be obedient to God than to be concerned with survival.

Perhaps the words of William Arthur Word will encourage us to quit "surviving" and therefore lose our fear of failure. "If you are wise, you will forget yourself into greatness. Forget your rights, but remember your responsibilities. Forget your inconveniences, but remember your blessings. Forget your own accomplishments, but remember your debts to others. Forget your privileges, but remember your obligations. Follow the examples of Florence Nightingale, of Albert Schweitzer, of Abraham Lincoln, of Tom Dooley, and forget yourself into greatness. If you are wise, you will empty yourself into adventure. Remember the words of General Douglas MacArthur: 'There is no security on this earth. There is only opportunity.' Empty your days of the search for security; fill them with a passion for service. Empty your hours of the ambition for recognition; fill them with the aspiration for achievement. Empty your moments of the need for entertainment; fill them with the quest for creativity. If you are wise, you will lose yourself into immortality. Lose your cynicism. Lose your doubts. Lose your fears. Lose your anxiety. Lose your unbelief. Remember these truths: A son must soon forget himself to be long remembered. He must empty himself in order to discover a fuller self. He must lose himself to find himself. Forget yourself into greatness. Empty yourself into adventure. Lose yourself into immortality."

Take a risk. Climb out on the limb where the fruit is. Too many people are still hugging the tree trunk, wondering why they are not receiving the fruit of life. Many potential leaders never achieved because they stood back and let someone else take the risk. Many potential recipients never did receive because they didn't step out of the crowd and ask. James tells us "we have not because we ask not." Realistically, we ask not because we fear rejection. Therefore we take no risk.

> *To laugh is to risk appearing the fool.*
> *To weep is to risk appearing sentimental.*
> *To reach out for another is to risk involvement.*
> *To expose feeling is to risk exposing your true self.*
> *To place your ideas, your dreams, before the crowd is to risk their loss.*
> *To love is to risk not being loved in return.*
> *To live is to risk dying.*
> *To hope is to risk despair.*
> *To try is to risk failure.*
> *—Author unknown*

But risk must be taken, because the greatest hazard in life is to risk nothing. The person who risks nothing, does nothing, has nothing and is nothing. He may avoid suffering and sorrow, but he simply cannot learn, grow, feel, change, love, live. Chained by his certitudes, he is a slave, he has forfeited freedom.

Fear of failure grips those who take themselves too seriously. While we were growing up, many of us spent a great deal of time worrying about what the world thinks of us. By the time we reach middle age we realize that the world wasn't paying much attention all the time we were worrying. Until we accept the fact that the future of the world does not hinge on our decisions, we will be unable to forget past mistakes.

In his autobiography, *The Tumult and the Shouting*, the great sports columnist Grantland Rice gives this advice about past mistakes.

"Because golf exposes the flaws of the human swing—a basically simple maneuver—it causes more self-torture than any game short of Russian roulette. The quicker the average golfer can forget the shot he had dubbed or knocked off-line—and concentrate on the next shot—the sooner he begins to improve and enjoy golf. Like life, golf can be humbling. However, little good comes from brooding about mistakes we've made. The next shot, in golf or life, is the big one."

Attitude is the determining factor of whether our failures

make or break us. The persistence of a person who encounters failure is one sign of a healthy attitude. Winners don't quit! Failure becomes devastating and causes our attitude to crash when we quit. To accept failure as final is to be finally a failure.

Everyone within range of the golden arches is aware of the success of McDonald's restaurants. The executives of this franchise followed a statement that said, "Press on. Nothing in the world can take the place of persistence. Talent will not; nothing in the world is more common than unsuccessful men with talent. Genius will not; the world is full of educated derelicts. Persistence and determination alone are omnipotent."

In times of failures a key is to look at our Creator and chief motivator.

WHEN IT LOOKS LIKE I HAVE FAILED

Lord, are you trying to tell me something?
For ...
Failure does not mean I'm a failure;
    It does mean I have not yet succeeded.
Failure does not mean I have accomplished nothing;
    It does mean I have learned something.
Failure does not mean I have been a fool;
    It does mean I had enough faith to experiment.
Failure does not mean I've been disgraced;
    It does mean I dared to try.
Failure does not mean I don't have it;
    It does mean I have to do something in a different way.
Failure does not mean I am inferior;
    It does mean I am not perfect.
Failure does not mean I've wasted my time;
    It does mean I have an excuse to start over.
Failure does not mean I should give up;
    It does mean I must try harder.
Failure does not mean I'll never make it;
    It does mean I need more patience.
Failure does not mean you have abandoned me;
    It does mean you must have a better idea. Amen.

Attitude Application:

Read these reinforcing thoughts about dealing with failure. Write them on a 3" x 5" card and keep them visible so you can read them often.

The man who never made a mistake never made anything.

84

Failures, repeated failures, are fingerprints on the road to achievement.

It is impossible to succeed without suffering.

"I don't have to survive."

Attitude is the determining factor of whether our failures make or break us.

To accept failure as final is to be finally a failure.

Failure is the line of least persistence.

The second storm within us that causes attitude crash is: *The Dread of Discouragement.*

Elijah is one of my favorite Bible characters. Never has a man of God enjoyed a greater moment then his experience at Mt. Carmel. Boldness, faith, power, obedience and effective prayer describes Elijah as he stood with the worshippers of Baal. But deliverance in 1 Kings 18 was followed by discouragement in 1 Kings 19. His attitude went from boldness before God to blaming God for his trouble. Fear replaced faith. Power was drained by pity, and disobedience replaced obedience. How quickly things changed. Sound familiar? Turn to 1 Kings 19 and notice the four thoughts on discouragement.

First, discouragement hurts our self-image. "But he himself went on a day's journey into the wilderness, and came and sat down under a juniper tree; and he requested for himself that he might die, and said, 'It is enough; now, O Lord, take my life, for I am not better than my fathers'" (v. 4).

Discouragement causes us to see ourselves as less than we really are. This fact becomes even more important when we realize that we cannot consistently perform in a manner that is inconsistent with the way we see ourselves.

Second, discouragement causes us to evade our responsibilities. "Then he came there to a cave, and lodged there; and behold, the word of the Lord came to him, and He said to him. 'What are you doing here, Elijah?'" (v. 9).

The Elijahs of life are created for Mt. Carmels, not caves. Faith brings us to ministry. Fear hands us only misery.

Third, discouragement causes us to blame others for our predicament. "And he said, 'I have been very zealous for the Lord, the God of hosts; for the sons of Israel have forsaken

Thy covenant, torn down Thine altars and killed Thy prophets with the sword. And I alone am left; and they seek my life, to take it away'" (v. 10).

Fourth, discouragement causes us to blur the facts. "Yet I will leave 7,000 in Israel, all the knees that have not bowed to Baal and every mouth that has not kissed him" (v. 18). From "only one" to "7,000." No doubt about it, discouragement had "done a number" on this great prophet. And if it can happen to great men, what about us? What about others? Discouragement is contagious.

You may have heard the story of the fellow who was about to jump from a bridge. An alert police officer slowly, methodically moved toward him, talking with him all the time. When the officer got within inches of the man he said, "Surely nothing could be bad enough for you to take your life. Tell me about it. Talk to me." The would-be jumper told how his wife had left him, how his business had gone bankrupt, how his friends had deserted him. Everything in life had lost meaning. For 30 minutes he told the sad story—then they both jumped!

We are all subject to the currents of discouragement that can sweep us into a danger zone. If we know some of the causes of discouragement we can more easily avoid it. Discouragement comes when we:

1. Feel that opportunity for success is gone.

The test of your character is seeing what it takes to stop you. We need the spirit of the boy in the little league. A man stopped to watch a little league baseball game. He asked one of the youngsters the score.

"We're behind 18 to nothing," was the answer.

"Well," said the man, "I must say you don't look discouraged."

"Discouraged?" the boy asked. "Why should we be discouraged? We haven't come to bat yet."

2. Become selfish.

Usually people who are discouraged are thinking mainly about one thing—themselves.

3. Are not immediately successful in our attempts to do something.

A study conducted by the National Retail Dry Goods Association points out that unsuccessful first attempts lead almost half of all salesmen to certain failure. Note:

48% of all salesmen make one call and stop.
25% of all salesmen make two calls and stop.
15% of all salesmen make three calls and stop.
12% of all salesmen go back and back and back and back.
They make 80% of all sales.

I witnessed the reality of this while pastoring at Faith Memorial Church in Lancaster, Ohio. We had several bus routes and picked up hundreds of people for church on Sunday. Each bus had a captain that would call on regular and potential riders each Saturday. Designated boundaries marked the geographical area for each route. The captains were not allowed to leave their "territory" to find new riders.

Evelyn McFarland was a successful captain. She averaged more than fifty rides per Sunday! Her secret? She did not take no for an answer. Every Saturday she would call on each house to possibly secure another rider. Her visits were recorded in a diary. On one page she had written, "I have visited this home over ninety times. Finally, today they said yes." Evelyn understood that we do not conquer through brilliance. We conquer by continuing!

4. Lack of purpose and a plan.

Another characteristic of discouragement is inactivity. You seldom see a discouraged activist running to and fro trying to help others. When you are discouraged, you tend to withdraw. Many times discouragement comes right after a successful venture. Elijah found this to be true. Perhaps he needed another Mt. Carmel to lift his spirits. When we lack a purpose, many times we lack fulfillment.

Thomas Edison's life was filled with purpose. When he spoke about his success he said, "The most important factors of invention can be described in a few words. (1) They must consist of definite knowledge as to what one wishes to achieve. (2) One must fix his mind on that purpose with persistence and begin searching for that which he seeks, making use of all of the accumulated knowledge of the subject which he has or can acquire from others. (3) He must keep on searching no matter how many times he may meet with disappointment. (4) He must refuse to be influenced by the fact that somebody else may have tried the same idea without success. (5) He must keep himself sold on the idea that the solution of his problem exists somewhere, and that he will find it . . . .

"When a man makes up his mind to solve any problem, he may at first meet with dogged opposition, but if he holds on and keeps on searching he will be sure to find some sort of solution. The trouble with most people is that they quit before they start" (source unknown).

By this time you may be totally discouraged, thinking there is little you can do to overcome those feelings of frustration and inadequacy. But here are some steps you can take.

1. Positive action

Take action on the problem! The moment you are certain of the source of discouragement, get busy. Nothing delivers us from discouragement quicker than taking positive steps to solve the problem.

A poet tells of walking in his garden and seeing a bird's nest lying on the ground. The storm had swept through the tree and ruined the nest. While he mused sadly over the wreck of the bird home, he looked up and saw them building a new one in the branches.

2. Positive thinking

Recently I was reading a brief but stimulating biography of Thomas Edison written by his son. What an amazing character! Thanks to his genius, we enjoy the microphone, the phonograph, the incandescent light, the storage battery, talking movies and more than a thousand other inventions. But beyond all that, Edison was a man who refused to be discouraged. His contagious optimism affected all those around him.

His son recalled a freezing December night in 1914. Unfruitful experiments on the nickel-iron-alkaline storage battery, a 10-year project, had put Edison on a financial tightrope. He was still solvent only because of profits from movie and record production.

On that December evening the cry "fire!" echoed through the plant. Spontaneous combustion had broken out in the film room. Within minutes all the packing compounds, celluloid for records and film and other flammable goods were burning. Fire companies from eight surrounding towns arrived, but the heat was so intense and the water pressure so low that attempts to douse the flames were futile. Everything was being destroyed.

When he couldn't find his father, the son became concerned. Was he safe? With all his assets being destroyed, would his spirit be broken? Soon he saw his father in the plant yard running toward him.

"Where's Mom?" shouted the inventor. "Go get her, son! Tell her to hurry up and bring her friends! They'll never see a fire like this again!"

Early the next morning, long before dawn, with the fire barely under control, Edison called his employees together and made an incredible announcement. "We're rebuilding!"

He told one man to lease all the machine shops in the area. He told another to obtain a wrecking crane from the Erie Railroad Company. Then, almost as an afterthought, he added, "Oh, by the way, anybody know where we can get some money?"

Later, he explained, "We can always make capital out of a disaster. We've just cleared out a bunch of old rubbish. We'll build bigger and better on the ruins." Shortly after that, he yawned, rolled up his coat for a pillow, curled up on a table and immediately fell asleep.

3. Positive example

It happened in Southwest Asia in the 14th Century. The army of Asian conqueror Emperor Tamerlane (a descendant of Ghengis Khan) had been routed, dispersed by a powerful enemy. Tamerlane himself lay hidden in a deserted manger while enemy troops scoured the countryside.

As he lay there, desperate and dejected, Tamerlane watched an ant try to carry a grain of corn over a perpendicular wall. The kernel was larger than the ant itself. As the emperor counted, sixty-nine times the ant tried to carry it up the wall. Sixty-nine times he fell back. On the seventieth try he pushed the grain of corn over the top.

Tamerlane leaped to his feet with a shout! He, too, would triumph in the end! And he did, reorganizing his forces and putting the enemy to flight.

4. Positive persistence

> Two frogs fell into a can of cream
> —or so I've heard it told
> The sides of the can were shiny and steep,
> the cream was deep and cold.
> "Oh, what's the use?" said No. 1,
> "'tis fate—no help's around—
> Good-bye, my friend! Good-bye, sad world!"
> And weeping still, he drowned.
> But No. 2 of sterner stuff,
> dog paddled in surprise,
> The while he wiped his creamy face
> and dried his creamy eyes.
> "I'll swim awhile, at least," he said
> —or so it has been said—
> "It wouldn't really help the world
> if one more frog was dead."
> An hour or two he kicked and swam—
> not once he stopped to mutter,
> But kicked and swam, and swam and kicked,
> then hopped out, via buttter.
>   —Author unknown

Too many times we become discouraged and accept defeat. One of the most famous race horses of all time was Man o' War. As a two-year-old, Man o' War won six consecutive races. Then in 1919, the champ came across a contender appropriately named Upset. For the first time in his life, Man o'War trailed another horse across the finish line.

As is often the case when a champion goes down in defeat, there were the usual circumstances that affected the situation. On this occasion, an assistant starter was working the gate at the Saratoga race track, and the break from the barrier was delayed for about five minutes. The champ, always nervous at the post, was dancing and bobbing his head, and when the field broke, the big red horse was off sideways, fifth in a seven-horse race.

A champion does not give up easily, and Man o' War was no exception. He made a gallant try to close the gap. By the time the race reached the halfway mark, the champ had already moved up to the fourth position. He had gained the third position by the three-quarter mark. At the turn into the stretch, he

90

moved clearly into second place. Ten lengths from home and he was "nodding at Upset's saddle girth." Given another two or three lengths, Man o' War would have been a clear winner. But Upset won by the narrowest possible margin.

When you read about that incident, you wish that the upset by Upset would never have happened.

You wish, too, that upsets some great men have experienced would never have happened, either. Abraham failed in an hour of emergency, and in weakness let a king think his wife, Sarah, was his sister. There is Jacob, who tricked his brother out of his own birthright; Moses, whose impatience lost him the right to enter the promised land; and David, that "man after God's own heart," who tarnished his name through adultery and murder. Elijah, too, was upset and prayed to die.

But—and this is what is most important of all—all of these men, after tragic upsets, went on to win great victories (as did Man o' War one year later, when he upset Upset).

Has some upsetting defeat or discouragement come your way recently? It's up to you to decide how you will handle the defeats of life. No man will go through all of life without meeting defeat from time to time. When it happens to you, don't quit! Missionary E. Stanley Jones said that he had adopted as his motto for life, "When life kicks you, let it kick you forward!" A wise resolve! Anyone can start but only a thoroughbred will finish!

Attitude Application:

Harold Sherman, quite awhile ago, wrote a book entitled, *How To Turn Failure Into Success.* In it he gives a *"Code of persistence."* If you give up too easily, write this down and read it daily:

1. I will never give up so long as I know I am right.
2. I will believe that all things will work out for me if I hang on until the end.
3. I will be courageous and undismayed in the face of odds.
4. I will not permit anyone to intimidate me or deter me from my goals.
5. I will fight to overcome all physical handicaps and setbacks.
6. I will try again and again and yet again to accomplish what I desire.

7. I will take new faith and resolution from the knowledge that all successful men and women have had to fight defeat and adversity.
8. I will never surrender to discouragement or despair no matter what seeming obstacles may confront me.

The third storm that rages within and causes our attitude to crash is: *The Struggle of Sin.*

"For that which I am doing, I do not understand; for I am not practicing what I would like to do, but I am doing the very thing I hate. But if I do the very thing I do not wish to do, I agree with the Law, confessing that it is good. So now, no longer am I the one doing it, but sin which indwells me. For I know that nothing good dwells in me, that is, in my flesh; for the wishing is present in me, but the doing of the good is not. For the good that I wish, I do not do; but I practice the very evil that I do not wish. But if I am doing the very thing I do not wish, I am no longer the one doing it, but sin which dwells in me. I find then the principle that evil is present in me, the one who wishes to do good. For I joyfully concur with the law of God in the inner man, but I see different law in the members of my body, waging war against the law of my mind, and making me a prisoner of the law of sin which is in my members. Wretched man that I am! Who will set me free from the body of this death? Thanks be to God through Jesus Christ our Lord! So then, on the one hand I myself with my mind am serving the law of God, but on the other, with my flesh the law of sin" (Romans 7:15-25).

Paul is not a golfer describing his inconsistent game. Rather, he is writing about the conflict of two natures within him. One says "do good" while the other drags him down.

Recently a new Christian was sharing with me his frustration over not always doing what was right and what he intended. This disciplined individual asked, "Pastor, do you understand what I feel?" My reply, "Yes, and so did Paul." I turned to Romans 7 and started reading. He stopped me and asked, "Where is that Scripture? I will need to go back to it."

I hope he will also go to Romans 8 where Paul tells of deliverance. "There is therefore now no condemnation for those who are in Christ Jesus" (v. 1).

Psalm 51 is known as David's prayer for pardon after he became involved in the double sin of adultery and murder. In Psalm 32 David records how he felt during the time he was trying to cover up his sin. "When I kept silent about my sin, my body wasted away through my groaning all day long." For a year he tried to live with a bad conscience and a fallen attitude. Finally, after the prophet Nathan's confrontation, David prays to God for forgiveness. That prayer is rendered in Psalm 51:1-2: "Be gracious to me, O God, according to Thy lovingkindness; according to the greatness of Thy compassion blot out my transgressions. Wash me thoroughly from my iniquity, and cleanse me from my sin." He then lays hold of forgiveness by acknowledging his guilt, recognizing his sin and not blaming God (vs. 3-4).

Forgiveness is one thing; however, overcoming sin is another. David prays for purifying power in verses 5 to 13. His prayer reveals eight steps to this deliverance and the power over sin.

1. "Help me to understand the truth about myself."

   "Behold, Thou dost desire truth in the innermost being, and in the hidden part Thou wilt make me know wisdom" (v. 6).

2. "Allow the blood sacrifice to be applied to my heart."

   "Purify me with hyssop, and I shall be clean; wash me, and I shall be whiter than snow" (v. 7).

3. "Fill me with joy and gladness."

   "Make me to hear joy and gladness, let the bones which Thou has broken rejoice" (v. 8).

4. "God, remember my sins no more. I can't always have them thrown up to me."

   "Hide Thy face from my sins, and blot out all my iniquities" (v. 9).

5. "Give me a new heart which naturally does good."

   "Create in me a clean heart, O God, and renew a steadfast spirit within me" (v. 10).

6. David needs and asks for continued assurance.

   "Do not cast me away from Thy presence, and do not take Thy Holy Spirit from me" (v. 11).

7. "Give me a will that wants to do what you want me to do."

"Restore to me the joy of Thy salvation, and sustain me with a willing spirit" (v. 12).

8. "Allow me to teach others what I have experienced."

"Then I will teach transgressors Thy ways, and sinners will be converted to Thee" (v. 13).

Susanna Wesley, mother of John and Charles, once used this striking sentence: "Whatever weakens your reason, impairs the tenderness of your conscience, obscures your sense of God, or removes your relish for spiritual things—that is sin to you."

Your attitude begins to falter when sin enters your life. A withdrawal, a hardness and a fleshly nature begin to invade us, all caused by sin. It is first appealing, then appalling; first alluring, then alienating; first deceiving, then damning; it promises life and produces death; it is the most disappointing thing in the world.

Understanding the problem is a good first step in correcting your perspective. If your attitude is threatening to crash, check the internal indications. See if you are afraid of failure, dealing with discouragement or struggling with sin.

10

THE CRASH FROM WITHOUT

Murphy's Law—"Nothing is as easy as it looks; everything takes longer than you expect; and if anything can go wrong, it will and at the worst possible moment."

Maxwell's Law—"Nothing is as hard as it looks; everything is more rewarding than you expect; and if anything can go right, it will and at the best possible moment."

INTERNAL PROBLEMS are not the only things that endanger our perspective. Our attitude sometimes crashes when the storms around us begin to take their toll. I have pinpointed four of these outward causes.

I call the first one *The Closeness of Criticism.*

I use the word "closeness" because the criticism that hurts always comes close to where we live or what we love. Others' criticism of us is like having someone "step on our blue suede shoes."

When speaking on this subject, many times I ask the audience if they can remember a critical statement that greatly affected their lives. I usually receive a unanimous "yes."

I too have heard my share of critical comments. I grew up in a denomination that placed a high status on pastors who received yearly unanimous votes of confidence from their congregations. Conversation during summer church conferences centered on the most recent votes. This emphasis was firmly implanted in my mind, and my prayer for my first pastorate was, "Oh Lord, help me to please everybody." (That is definitely a prayer for failure.) I did my best. I kissed the babies, visited the elderly, married the young, buried the dead, everything I thought I should do. Finally the annual vote was to be taken on my performance. Fifteen years later I still remember the results! Thirty-one yes, one no, and one abstention. Now what would you do? Not everyone was pleased with me. I rushed to the phone and called my father for his advice. Fortunately he reassured me that the church would make it through the "crisis." Unfortunately, for six months I wondered who voted no.

From that early pastoral experience I learned the negative effect that criticism can have on a young church leader. A person entering his calling with a dream can easily be crushed unless he understands that the best fruit is the one the birds pick.

Jesus, perfect in love and motives, was criticized and misunderstood continually. People:

> called Him a glutton in Matthew 11:19;
> called Him a winebibber in Luke 7:34;
> criticized Him for associating with sinners in Matthew 9:11;
> accused Him of being a Samaritan, and of having a demon,
>   in John 8:48.

In spite of experiencing misunderstanding, ingratitude and rejection, our Lord never became bitter, discouraged or overcome. To Him every obstacle was an opportunity. Brokenheartedness? An opportunity to comfort. Disease? An opportunity to heal. Hatred? An opportunity to love. Temptation? An opportunity to overcome. Sin? An opportunity to forgive. Jesus always turned trials into triumphs.

Contrast that with the attitude of Amos on radio's old "Amos 'n' Andy" show. Amos was tired of Andy's constant criticism. Most irritating was Andy's finger continually thumping on Amos' chest. One day Amos could take no more. He bought some dynamite, taped it to his chest and told his friend Kingfish. "The next time Andy starts criticizing and thumping his fingers on my chest, this dynamite is going to blow his hand off!" Of course, he didn't stop to think of what it would do to his precious chest.

We always hurt ourselves when our reaction toward those who criticize us becomes negative. When such feelings arise, it is important to read the teachings of Jesus.

> You have heard that it was said, "You shall love your neighbor, and hate your enemy." But I say to you, love your enemies, and pray for those who persecute you in order that you may be sons

of your Father who is in heaven; for He causes the sun to rise on the evil and the good, and sends rain on the righteous and un-righteous. For if you love those who love you, what reward have you? Do not even the tax-gatherers do the same? And if you greet brothers only, what do you do more than others? Do not even the Gentiles do the same? Therefore you are to be perfect, as your heavenly Father is perfect (Matthew 5:43-48).

Attitude Application:

Here are some ways to keep criticism from sabotaging your attitude.

1. When possible, avoid people who belittle you. Small people try to tear you down, but big people make you feel worth-while.

2. Ask yourself: What bothers me most when I am criticized? Who says it? Why was it said? What was the attitude that ac-companied it; the place where it was shared? Is criticism com-ing from different people about the same subject? Is it valid? If so, am I doing anything about it?

3. Find a friend who has the gift of encouragement. Go to him and receive healing from his gift. But never receive his support without using your gift to minister in return.

The second storm is *The Presence of Problems.*

A couple's only son had been sent away to college. Their expectations were high, but his grades were low. After a few months the collegian was kicked out of school. Knowing the disappointment that his parents would feel, he sent his mother a telegram that read, "Flunked all my courses—kicked out of school—coming home—prepare Pop."

The next day he received the following telegram: "Pop pre-pared—prepare yourself."

Life is full of such problems and we might as well be pre-pared for them. There is no such place as a trouble-free area and no such person as one who knows no problems. And Chris-tians aren't exempt!

It is my responsibility and joy to disciple the lay leaders of my congregation. Most recently, we have been studying 2 Tim-othy in a series I call "Time Out for Timothy." One subject was "Persecution of the Christian Leader." The central thought: "All who desire to live godly lives in Christ Jesus will be persecuted." The major question discussed in this study was, "Can you name a Bible character greatly used of God who did not endure trials?" Take a moment and try it. Almost without exception, the people we read about in God's word encountered troubles.

> "When Noah sailed the waters blue
> He had his troubles same as you;
> For forty days he drove the ark
> Before he found a place to park."

At times we all become "flooded" with problems. Perhaps it is the number of difficulties more than the size of any one trouble that wears us down. We all have moments when we "bite off more than we can chew."

There are more moments when we feel like the lion tamer who had more than he could handle and put the following ad in a show business paper: "Lion tamer—wants tamer lion."

The ad underscores the feeling of the man in the following story. He was one of those persons who accepted everything that happened as a manifestation of a divine power. It was not for him, he said, to question the workings of a Divine Providence.

All his life misfortune had been his, yet never once did he complain. He married, and his wife ran away with the hired man. He had a daughter, and the daughter was deceived by a villain. He had a son, and the son was lynched. A fire burned down his barn, a cyclone blew away his home, a hailstorm destroyed his crops, and the banker foreclosed on his mortgage, taking his farm. Yet at each fresh stroke of misfortune he knelt and gave thanks to God Almighty for His interminable mercy.

After a time, penniless, but still submissive to the decrees from on high, he landed in the county poorhouse. One day the overseer sent him out to plow a potato field. A thunderstorm came up but seemed to be passing over when, without warning, a bolt of lightning descended from the sky. It melted the plowshare, stripped most of his clothing from him, singed off his beard, branded his naked back with the initials of a neighboring cattleman and hurled him through a barbed wire fence.

When he recovered consciousness, he got slowly to his knees, clasped his hands and raised his eyes toward heaven.

Then, for the first time, he asserted himself: "Lord," he said, "this is gettin' to be plumb ridiculous!"

At a moment like this our attitude has a tendency to crash. When that happens we have two alternatives. We can either alter the difficulty or alter ourselves. What can be changed for the best, we must change. When that is impossible, we must adjust to the circumstances in a positive way.

Before the days of antibiotics, Robert Louis Stevenson, the great Scottish novelist and author of *Treasure Island*, was bedridden with consumption a great deal. Still, the disease never stifled his optimism. Once when his wife heard him coughing badly, she said to him: "I expect you still believe it's a wonderful day."

Stevenson looked at the rays of sunshine bouncing off the walls of his bedroom, then replied: "I do. I will never permit a row of medicine bottles to block my horizon."

The apostle Paul possessed the same attitude. He said, "We are pressed on every side by troubles, but not crushed and broken. We are perplexed because we don't know why things happen as they do, but we don't give up and quit. We are hunted down, but God never abandons us. We get knocked down, but we get up again and keep going (2 Corinthians 4:8,9, Living Bible).

Attitude Application:

What are problems?

PREDICTORS—They help mold our future.

REMINDERS—We are not self-sufficient. We need God and others to help.

OPPORTUNITIES—They pull us out of our rut and cause us to think creatively.

BLESSINGS—They open up doors that we usually do not go through.

LESSONS—Each new challenge will be our teacher.

EVERYWHERE—No place or person is excluded from them.

MESSAGES—They warn us about potential disaster

SOLVEABLE—No problem is without a solution.

They are everywhere—no place or person is excluded from them.

The third external storm that can cause our attitude to fall is *The Conflict of Change.*

We resist nothing more than change. Many times we enjoy the rewards of change, but endure its process. We are creatures of habit. We first form habits, then our habits form us. We are what we repeatedly do. It is easy to see "our world" only from our perspective. When that occurs, we stagnate and become narrow. If all you have is a hammer then everything looks like a nail.

Read the following statements. One is always true. The other is not.

"Change brings growth."
"Growth brings change."

The first statement, "change brings growth," is true only if your attitude is right. With the proper attitude, all change, whether positive or negative will be a learning experience which results in a growing experience.

Our inability to control changing situations has caused many attitudes to crash. Yet this does not have to happen. Last Christmas I was walking through our church offices wishing everyone a merry Christmas. Stopping to speak to one of the volunteer secretaries, I asked, "Are you ready for Christmas?" With a smile she replied, "Almost, just one more Care Bear to stuff." Figuring she was making the bears for her grandchildren, I asked, "How many grandchildren do you have?" "None," she replied. "But that's okay. I went out into my neighborhood and adopted some. I figured that if I'm going to have a family at Christmas, then I'd better go round them up!"

With a little coaxing from me, she began to explain some of the problems she'd had with her own family. The more she told me, the more I sensed that this remarkable lady had refused to wallow in the pool of pity in which so many are drowning. Christmas to her would be lovely and not lonely only because she would not allow her attitude to crash over things she could not control.

Dr. G. Campbell Morgan tells of a man whose shop had been burned in the great Chicago fire. He arrived at the ruins the next morning carrying a table. He set it up amid the charred debris and above it placed this optimistic sign, "Everything lost except wife, children, and hope. Business will be resumed as usual tomorrow morning."

Sadly, too many are like the old man in northern Maine who had turned 100. A New York reporter who went up to interview him commented, "I'll bet you have seen a lot of changes in your 100 years."

The elderly fellow crossed his arms, jutted his jaw and replied with indignation, "Yes, and I've been agin' every one of them!"

I have spent much time observing why and when people start resisting change. Some strive until they are comfortable, then they settle in and don't want to grow. For most, a negative experience has made them pull back and say "never again."

At a coastal aquarium, a savage barracuda quickly tried to attack the mackerel but was stopped by the partition. After bumping his nose repeatedly, he finally quit trying. Later, the partition was removed, but the barracuda would swim only to the point where the barrier had been and stop. He thought it was still there! Many people are like this. They move forward until they reach an imaginary barrier, but then stop because of a self-imposed attitude of limitation.

If they only knew how unhealthy such an attitude is.

Change is essential for growth. A famous inventor once said, "The world hates change, yet it is the only thing that has brought progress." For the Christian, change should bring us closer to God. He has ordained change. We need to remind ourselves that not all people are born at the same time. God has ordained that there be a succession of generations: First a man is a son, then a father, then a grandfather and possibly even a great-grandfather. Each new generation is God's way of telling us that He still has purposes for us to fulfill. In fact, each generation has three specific functions to perform: (1) conserve, (2) criticize, (3) create.

Each generation is a bank in which the previous generation deposits its valuables. The new generation examines those valuables, rejects what is no longer needed and uses what is left to create new treasures. This whole process of conserving, criticizing and creating adds up to the one thing we fear: change.

Just suppose each new generation had to discover numerals or language, or medicine or the Gospel? The world would see no progress. But because each generation conserves what previous generations have discovered, we can continue to make progress in the important areas of life. This does not mean that each generation necessarily uses this conserved knowledge and skill for the best purposes, but it does mean that each new generation stands on the shoulders of the past and tries to reach higher.

When you realize that God has ordained new generations, and that new generations bring about change, you understand that one generation cannot do without the others. The older generation likes to conserve; the younger generation likes to criticize, but this interaction produces the friction that helps to generate the power for progress. The older generation is our link with the past, the younger generation is our link with the future, and we need both. The younger men need the wisdom of the older men, and the older men need the daring and the vision of the younger. To embalm the past is to turn society into a museum and destroy what future God has for us.

Even when people realize that change is inevitable, they respond differently to its challenges. Some retreat into their emotional and spiritual bombshelters and refuse to become a part of the action. One church member said to his pastor, "It's such a relief to come to a church where nothing has changed in 30 years!" My heart bleeds for that pastor. On the other hand, there are those who go to the other extreme and change with every new gust of wind. They jump from bandwagon to bandwagon, and, like the Athenians Paul preached to, they are always looking for some new thing. The old hymns are buried, the familiar forms of worship are laid to rest, and even the traditional terminology is replaced by a jargon that may leave the poor worshipper wondering whether even God understands what is going on.

Still, the right amount of change can strengthen us. Moses uses an interesting illustration in Deuteronomy 32:11, where he describes the mother eagle forcing her young to leave the nest and fly. The eaglet wants to stay in the nest and be fed, but if he remains there, he will never use his great wings or enjoy the great heights for which he was created. So, his mother has to knock him out of the nest, catch him on her wings when he falls too far and repeat the process until he learns to fly on his own.

You and I enjoy our little nests, and we have worked hard to build them. This explains why we resent it when God starts to "shake up" the nest. God wants us to grow! The timid souls pray, "Oh, that I had wings like a dove! I would fly away and be at rest" (Psalms 55:6).But the courageous souls claim Isaiah 40:31 and "mount up with wings as eagles" right in the face of the wind! Not everybody who grows old, grows up, and those who fail to grow up are often the ones who have run away from the challenge of change.

It is encouraging to see how many men and women God has used during what should have been their "comfortable years." Abraham and Moses were not young men when God called them, and just about the time Saul of Tarsus was settling down in his rabbinical career, God shook his nest and forced him to fly. Modern church and missionary history is filled with stories about mature people who willingly left the nest to serve God on eagles' wings.

The fourth storm, which causes more attitude fatalities than anything else, is what I call *The Night of Negativism.*

Our thoughts govern our actions. That is a fact. In Matthew 15:19, the Lord said, "For out of the heart come evil thoughts, murders, adulteries, fornications, thefts, false witness, slanders." The question is, "Are we governed by negative or positive thoughts?" As negative thoughts produce negative actions, so positive thoughts produce positive actions. Today we are where we are and what we are because of the thoughts that dominated our minds.

Paul realized the power of our thought life and in Philippians 4 encouraged us to let our minds dwell on "Whatever is true, whatever is honorable, whatever is right, whatever is pure, whatever is lovely, whatever is of good repute," and then only if these things are excellent and worthy of praise.

Our challenge is to think right in a negative world. Every day we receive news that is less than uplifting. We all know people who can hardly wait for the future so they can look back with regret. Asked by a market research firm, R.H. Brieskin Associates, to state the best thing that had happened to them in the past five years, 12 percent of the people surveyed answered, "nothing." These people can see only bad options in every situation. If they swallowed an egg they would be afraid to move for fear it would break, and afraid to sit for fear it would hatch. Negative thinking and living does many detrimental things to our life. Let's look at a few of them.

1. Negative thinking creates clouds at critical decision times.

We become tense instead of relaxing. Taking a test is an example of this. An often-heard comment while cramming is, "I hope they don't ask me that question. I'm sure I'll miss it." We start the test and sure enough, there is the question, followed by the predicted outcome. Accident? No. It's a prophecy fulfilled. You felt negative about the question, declared your fear and responded accordingly. Next time you're studying for an exam, say to yourself, "If there ever will be a time when I remember the answer to this question, it will be when I take the test."

2. Negative talking is contagious.

A man who lived by the side of the road and sold hot dogs was hard of hearing, so he had no radio. He had trouble with his eyes, so he read no newspapers. But he sold good hot dogs. He put up signs on the highway advertising them. He stood on the side of the road and cried, "Buy a hot dog, mister?" And people bought his hot dogs. He increased his meat and bun orders. He bought a bigger stove to take care of his trade.

He finally got his son to come home from college to help out. But then something happened. "Father, haven't you been listening to the radio?" his son said. "Haven't you been reading the newspaper? There's a big recession on. The European situation is terrible. The domestic situation is worse."

Whereupon the father thought, "Well, my son's been to college, he reads the papers and he listens to the radio, and he ought to know."

So the father cut down his meat and bun orders, took down his signs and no longer bothered to stand out on the highway to sell his hot dogs. His sales fell overnight.

"You're right, son," the father said to the boy. "We certainly are in the middle of a big recession."

Has someone else's negative attitude ever changed your actions?

3. Negative thinking blows everything out of proportion.

Some people treat the drip from a leaky roof like a hurricane. Everything is a major project. They find a problem in every solution.

Murphy's law states, "Nothing is as easy as it looks; everything takes longer than you expect; and if anything can go wrong, it will and at the worst possible moment."

Maxwell's Law states, "Nothing is as hard as it looks; everything is more rewarding than you expect; and if anything can go right, it will and at the best possible moment."

4. Negative thinking limits God and our potential.

One of the saddest stories in the Bible is about Israel's failure to enter the promised land as told in Numbers 13 and 14. It is a classic example of how a negative report can limit God and others.

Twelve spies went into Canaan under the same orders, to the same places, at the same time and came back with different advice. For Joshua and Caleb the promised land was everything that God said it would be. They reported, "It certainly does flow with milk and honey and this is its fruit."

The other ten men offered a negative report. In verses 28-29 of Chapter 13, they reported facts without faith. "Nevertheless, the people who live in the land are strong, and the cities are fortified and very large; and moreover, we saw the descendants of Anak there," they said. "Amalek is living in the land of the Negev and the Hittites and the Jebusites and the Amorites are living in the hill country, and the Canaanites are living by the sea and by the side of the Jordan."

In verse 31 we see that they had goals without God. "But the men who had gone up with him said, 'We are not able to go up against the people, for they are too strong for us.'"

Verses 32 and 33 tell us that they continued with exaggeration without encouragement. "So they gave out to the sons of Israel a bad report of the land which they had spied out, saying, 'The land through which we have gone, in spying it out, is a land that devours its inhabitants; and all the people whom we saw in it are men of great size. There also we saw the Nephilim (the sons of Anak are part of the Nephilim); and we became like grasshoppers in our own sight, and so we were in their sight.'"

The result? "Then all the congregation lifted up their voice and cried, and the people wept that night. And all the sons of Israel grumbled against Moses and Aaron; and the whole congregation said to them, 'Would that we had died in the land of Egypt! Or would that we had died in this wilderness! And why is the Lord bringing us into this land, to fall by the sword? Our wives and our little ones will become plunder; would it not be better for us to return to Egypt?' So they said to one another, 'Let us appoint a leader and return to Egypt'" (Numbers 14:1-4). They settled for second best!

5. Negative thinking keeps us from enjoying life.

A negative person expects nothing off a silver platter except tarnish. If you have a negative neighbor, borrow a cup of sugar from him. He never expects to be paid back. Chisolm, a thinker and the "father of this crowd" said, "Any time things appear to be getting better you have overlooked something."

6. Negative living hinders others from making a positive response.

This is probably the greatest danger of a negative lifestyle. It tends to control those you influence and love the most.

Even the answer to a question depends a great deal on how you ask it. As experienced salesmen have long known, questions phrased either positively or negatively usually elicit a corresponding reply.

For example, a young psychology student drafted into the Army decided to test this theory. Drawing K.P., he was given the job of passing out apricots at the end of the chow line.

"You don't want apricots, do you?" he asked the first few men. Ninety percent said, "No."

Then he tried the positive approach: "You do want some

apricots, don't you?" About half answered, "Uh, yeah, I'll take some."

Then he tried a third test, based on the fundamental either/or selling technique. "One dish of apricots, or two?" he asked. And in spite of the fact that most soldiers don't like Army apricots, 40 percent took two dishes and 50 percent took one!

The most common type of negativism that hinders others is characterized by what I call a "flat world" statement. This is a sincere statement that has been conditioned by past education and experience. It is not true, yet is accepted as fact. Therefore, it directs the thinking and action of many individuals.

History abounds with tales of experts who said positively that things could not be done—and were proven wrong. The classic "flat world" illustration is about Columbus and his plans for exploration.

In 1490 Queen Isabella and King Ferdinand of Spain commissioned a royal committee to look into Christopher Columbus' scheme to find a new and shorter route to the fabled Indies.

The committee, an impressive panel of experts headed by Spain's leading geographer and scholar, examined Columbus' plans and presented its findings to the King and Queen. The scheme could not be carried out. Quite impossible, they wrote.

Columbus had trouble financing his ships and convincing a crew to sail "around" the world. Why? He was fighting a cultural trance. Most of the people believed one thing and were not open to other possibilities. For Columbus, the problem was that everyone *knew* the earth was flat.

Fortunately, Isabella, Ferdinand and, more important, Columbus himself ignored the experts. The Nina, the Pinta and the little Santa Maria set sail and a flat world was found to be round. "Impossible" new lands became thriving and very "possible" places.

During the early 1900s an impressive array of scientific wizards pooh-poohed the idea of the airplane. Stuff and nonsense, they said. An opium-induced fantasy. A crackpot idea.

One of America's influential scientific journalists hurried to say, "Time and money is being wasted on aircraft experimentation."

One week later, on a bumpy field at a place called Kitty

Hawk, North Carolina, the Wright Brothers taxied their crackpot idea down a homemade runway and launched the human race into the air.

Even after that, the experts continued to snipe at the airplane.

Marshall Foch, Supreme Commander of the Allied Forces in France in World War I, watched a display and said, "All very well for sport, but it is no use whatsoever to the Army."

Thomas Edison is on record as having said that talking pictures would never catch on. "Nobody," he said, "would pay to listen to sounds coming from a screen."

He also tried to persuade Henry Ford to abandon his work on the fledgling idea of a motor car. "It's a worthless idea," Edison, persistent in his own endeavors, told the young Ford. "Come and work for me and do something really worthwhile."

Benjamin Franklin was told by experts to stop all that foolish experimenting with lightning. It was a waste of time, they said.

Madame Curie was urged, by experts, to forget the scientifically impossible idea of radium.

Laurence Olivier was earnestly advised by a sincere theatrical expert to give up plans for a career in the theater because he just did not have what it took to be a good actor.

No doubt, way back in the dim underside of time, a stubborn caveman kept insisting to his friends that he could start the world's first man-made fire. All around him, wise graybeards shook their heads and mumbled, "He's not all there. He's definitely a bit of a nut. Somebody ought to tell him that it just will not work."

Today we are still having difficulty with "flat world" people. Many of our accepted assumptions have a tendency to stifle creativity and the achievement of our true potential.

To crystalize our understanding of this subtle form of negativism I have listed some "flat world" statements.

"Leaders are born, not made."
"Nice guys finish last."
"It's not what you know, but who you know."
"You can't teach an old dog new tricks."

When we become conditioned to perceived truth and closed

to new positive possibilities the following happens:

> We *see* what we *expect* to see, not what we *can* see.
> We *hear* what we *expect* to hear, not what we *can* hear;
> We *think* what we *expect* to think, not what we *can* think.

Attitude Applications

How do you make your "flat world" round?

1. Identify the reason you are a "flat world" person
2. Identify the areas in which you think "flat world."
3. Identify people who can help you change this limiting thought process.
4. Continually check up on your progress.
5. Read and listen to positive self-help books and tapes.
6. Accept very few dogmatic, extreme statements.
7. Place all statements made into their proper context.
8. Take into account the source of the statement.
9. Remember, experience can limit your perspective rather than expand it.
10. What is possible is not always achieved quickly and endorsed enthusiastically.

Closing thought:
A "flat world" mind-set allows us to sleep on top of it.
A "round world" mind-set keeps us moving around it.

SECTION IV
THE CHANGING OF YOUR ATTITUDE

11

Up, Up, Up and Away

"Most people are very close to becoming the person that God wants them to be."

—*John Maxwell*

ONE OF THE GREAT discoveries we make, one of our great surprises, is to find we can do what we were afraid we couldn't do. Most of the prison bars we beat against are within us; we put them there and we can take them down.

Now that statement includes some good news and some bad news. The bad news is that we bring many of our problems on ourselves. The good news is that beginning today, we can "break out" of our prison of bad attitudes and become free for effective living.

This section is dedicated to clearly laying out a workable process to help you overcome an attitude problem. For this process to be successful, you should understand these statements.

1. The process takes a lot of dedication and work to be effective.

2. The process of change is never complete, therefore constant review of Section IV will insure the best results.

3. All excuses for wrong attitudes must be eliminated immediately. Face changing with the sincerity and honesty of the Negro spiritual that says, "It's me, it's me, it's me, oh Lord, standing in need of prayer."

4. Find a friend to whom you can be accountable on a regular basis for your change of attitude.

5. Remember, as you read these next pages, you are able to change any attitude you desire.

The individual's attitude is my major emphasis in conducting leadership conferences across the country. Most people are very close to becoming the person that God wants them to be. Continually I say to them and now to you, "You're only an attitude away!" My greatest joy is in helping hundreds of people change an attitude they feel "stuck with" for the rest of their lives. For your encouragement, a testimonial of a changed life, resulting from a changed attitude, is included in this chapter. Read this person's story and remember, this can happen to you.

"As a man thinks within himself, so he is" (Proverbs 23:7). This verse has special significance for me. I have personally experienced the influence of attitudes, for my thinking in life has produced two different men.

My conversion to Christ was the turning point for me. I changed from being a person with negative attitudes to one who lives with a positive mind-set. People see me as a very positive person today, but they would not have recognized me eleven years ago. My attitudes have come through a healing, reshaping, transforming process.

Before I was a Christian, my attitude was shaped by the world around me. My thinking was conformed to the world's values. I was reared in a broken home and was saturated with the attitude that life was a struggle, a fight for survival. I had a negative self-image because the significant people in my life (family, peers, etc.) possessed negative self-images. Criticism and negative thinking became my way of life because those attitudes were modeled by the people around me. Obstacles and problems were never seen as opportunities for growth. Problems were curses to be lived with, not blessings in disguise which could be solved.

I felt that life had dealt me a bad hand. I was doomed to have the "short end of the stick." I became self-centered and self-seeking. I wanted only to see what I could get from life. As I pursued this negative lifestyle, I found no fulfillment. Life itself seemed meaningless; it always had a dark cloud hanging over it.

The people I associated with, the literature I read, the music I listened to and my failure to know God, all shaped my attitudes in a non-positive way.

Christ came into my life at a very significant point. When I was most discouraged with living, He made me a new person. I began to see that "Christ in me" meant a transformation of my mind. I did not become a superpositive person overnight, but I began immediately to see life differently.

114

His Word within me, not the world around me, began to influence my attitudes. I made a willful choice to abide by God's Word. I had a battle with recurring, negative thoughts. But I desired with all my heart to be different. I wanted to be a positive person. I wanted to have the mind of Christ.

As I learned more about Christ, submitted to His will and obeyed His leading, I found my bitterness toward life changed. Life became a blessing, not a burden. Life was full of opportunities, not obstacles.

I purposely set out to expose myself to positive role models. I read positive-thinking books, listened to positive people, associated with positive groups. Please be aware that these changes were not always easy. I had to battle the old thinking sometimes. But the grace of God was the key factor in transforming my attitude.

I know that God can help anyone change their attitude. He changed my attitude toward life from that of positive, edifying, other-centered, Christ-directed living. I believe the key factors in my attitude transformation were faith in God, desire to change, willingness to do what was needed to be different (associate with different people, etc.) and a strong resolve to be positive each day.

I used to believe that circumstances determined my attitude. But I now know that choice, not circumstances, determines how I think. Anyone can become a positive person, if he wants to be. God will help all who desire to be different.

The process I've been through has been exciting. It's still going on. God is faithful. The work He has begun, He will finish. We don't have to remain negative people. We can be positive—if we want to submit ourselves to the process of change.

Certainly this man has undergone some tremendous changes. Every time I read his personal testimony I sense much positive growth in his life. Fortunately, he is a close friend and I have been able also to see the success of his new, positive attitude. When change is successful, we look back and call it growth.

Most people who have negative attitudes do not realize that attitudes know no barriers. The only barriers that bring our attitudes into bondage are those we place upon them. Attitudes, like faith, hope and love, can cross over any obstacle. Realizing this truth, let me encourage you to take control of your attitudes and begin the needed changes.

The pilot of an aircraft understands that he sets the attitude of the plane. He determines the direction of the attitude. The results follow. Climbing to a higher altitude takes time. Radio and television commentator Paul Harvey said, "You can tell when you are on the road to success. It's uphill all the way." It will take time to reach new heights. Be patient, knowing that anything worthwhile is worth working for. Although change itself is not progress, it is the price that we pay for progress.

Before you begin the process of change, here is a prayer for you:

Dear God,
    Change is never easy, yet growth demands it.
    Therefore, I fearfully step out of my world of defeatism and cautiously open myself to a world of winners.
    It will take time, Lord.
    Therefore, I will be patient in letting You and others help me become "perfect and complete, lacking in nothing" (James 1:4).
    I will need a lot of help.
    Therefore, I will accept those You send to me from various places at various times for my specific needs.
    Truthfully, Father, I'm still intimidated and lack strength.
    Therefore, I ask that You will do something for me that I cannot do for myself.
    And as my attitudes change and a "better me" becomes a reality, I will give you all the praise. Amen.

12

THE CHOICE WITHIN YOU

"Take one giant step at a time. Military strategists teach their armies to fight on one front at a time. Settle on one attitude you want to tackle at this time."

—*John Maxwell*

WE ARE EITHER THE masters or the victims of our attitudes. It is a matter of personal choice. Who we are today is the result of choices made yesterday. Tomorrow we will become what we choose today. To change means to choose to change.

In the Canadian northlands there are just two seasons, winter and July. When the back roads begin to thaw, they become muddy. Vehicles going into the backwood country leave deep ruts that become frozen when cold weather returns. For those entering this primitive area during the winter months, there is a sign which reads, "Driver, please choose carefully which rut you drive in, because you'll be in it for the next twenty miles."

Please follow carefully the course that you chart for your change of attitude. "Twenty miles" down the road you'll be glad you did. Only you can determine to take the steps as outlined in this chapter. They are not only the first steps that must be taken, but they are also the most important. Without taking these, it will be impossible to take the others.

Choice #1—Evaluate your present attitudes.

This will take some time. If possible, try to separate yourself from your attitudes. The goal of this exercise is not to see the "bad you" but a "bad attitude" that keeps you from being a more fulfilled person. The evaluation helps you make key changes only when you identify the problem.

117

When he sees a log jam, the professional logger climbs a tall tree and locates a key log, blows it up and lets the stream do the rest. An amateur would start at the edge of the jam and move all the logs, eventually moving the key log. Obviously, both methods will get the logs moving, but the professional does his work more quickly and effectively. Results are the only real reason for activity. The following evaluation process is developed to help you search for the right answers in the most efficient way.

Stages of Evaluation:

1. IDENTIFY PROBLEM FEELINGS—What attitudes make you feel the most negative about yourself? Usually feelings can be sensed before the problem is clarified. Write them down.
2. IDENTIFY PROBLEM BEHAVIOR—What attitudes cause you the most problems when dealing with others? Write them down.
3. IDENTIFY PROBLEM THINKING—We are the sum of our thoughts. "As a man thinks within himself, so he is." What thoughts consistently control your mind? Although this is the beginning step in correcting attitude problems, these are not as easy to identify as the first two.
4. CLARIFY BIBLICAL THINKING—What do the Scriptures teach about you as a person and about your attitudes? Later in this section I will share a scriptural view of right attitudes.
5. SECURE COMMITMENT—"What must I do to change?" now becomes "I must change." Remember, the choice to change is the one decision that must be made, and only you can do it.
6. PLAN AND CARRY OUT YOUR CHOICE—This is the process that Section IV is helping you accomplish.

Suggestion:

This evaluation will take time. If you have an encouraging friend who knows you well, perhaps you should enlist his help.

Choice #2—Realize that faith is stronger than fear.

The only thing that will guarantee the success of a doubtful undertaking is the faith from the beginning that you can do it. Jesus said, "If you have faith, and do not doubt, you shall ... say to this mountain, 'Be taken up and cast into the sea,' it shall be done" (Matthew 21:21).

There is a biblical way to handle fear so that an endeavor can be successful and not be limited by it. The early church in

Acts was experiencing tremendous growth. However, in Acts 4, Christians came up against some stiff opposition. They were commanded to stop witnessing or suffer severe consequences. Together they withdrew to pray. Verses 29-31 record a process they underwent to handle their fear. As you approach changing attitudes, this formula for fear will be helpful.

Four-step Formula to Handle Fear

1. Understand that God sees your problems.

"And now, Lord, take note of their threats ... " (v. 29). These who encountered difficulties wanted the assurance that God had seen their persecution. When things are going well, we do not need constant assurance that God is with us. But during battle (and you will have battles) there is a strong need for security. The good news is, God Himself has said, "I will never desert you, nor will I ever forsake you."

2. Ask for a filling of confidence and love that is greater than fear.

"Grant that Thy bond-servants may speak Thy word with all confidence" (v. 29). This was a request for more positive things to fill their hearts and minds. They realized that an effective way to experience less fear was to have more courage. It is unrealistic to think that all apprehensions, questions and intimidations will flee and never haunt us again. Usually both positive and negative are at work in our lives at the same time. The secret to overcoming? Possess stronger positive emotions and seek stronger positive reinforcement than negative.

3. Believe God is working a miracle in your life.

" ... while Thou dost extend Thy hand to heal, and signs and wonders take place through the name of Thy holy servant Jesus" (v. 30). Now there was a prayer for God to intercede on their behalf with miracles. They realized that what had to be done would take their effort plus God's. Notice they asked for strength first, and then they requested that God would make up the difference.

This must happen in your life. Place the changes you seek in attitude, thinking and behavior at the top of your prayer list. Ask God to help you do what is possible to bring about effective change. Then, ask Him to do for you what you cannot do for yourself.

4. Be filled with the Holy Spirit.

"And when they had prayed, the place where they had gathered together was shaken, and they were all filled with the Holy Spirit, and began to speak the word of God with boldness" (v. 31). There is a definite relationship between the filling of the Holy Spirit and boldness. Later in this section, more emphasis will be given to the need for Spirit-filled living.

I know many people who use this four-step formula to handle fear on a daily basis. It guards them and imparts strength. I encourage you to continually refer to this formula when fears begin to hinder your progress.

You are now preparing to take a big step. Don't be fearful or hesitant. You can't cross a chasm in two small jumps. The future is worth the risk. Tomorrow you will look back at the changes and call them improvements.

Years ago a small town in Maine was proposed for the site of a great hydro-electric plant. Since a dam would be built across the river, the town would be submerged. When the project was announced, the people were given many months to arrange their affairs and relocate.

During the time before the dam was built, an interesting thing happened. All improvements ceased! No painting was done. No repairs were made on the buildings, roads and sidewalks. Day by day the whole town got shabbier and shabbier. A long time before the waters came, the town looked uncared for and abandoned, even though the people had not yet moved away. One citizen explained: "Where there is no faith in the future, there is no power in the present." That town was cursed with hopelessness because it had no future.

Choice #3—Write a statement of purpose.

One day Charlie Brown was in his back yard having target practice with his bow and arrows. He would pull the bow string back and let the arrow fly into a fence. Then he would go to where the arrow had landed and draw a target around it. Several arrows and targets later, Lucy said to Charlie Brown, "You don't have target practice that way. You draw the target, then shoot the arrow." Charlie's response: "I know that, but, if you do it my way, you never miss!"

Sadly, many people approach their lives like Charlie Brown shoots arrows. They never draw a target and they never miss their goal. But they never hit one either.

When I was a boy, my father decided to build a basketball court for my brother and me. He made a cement driveway, put a backboard on the garage and was just getting ready to put up the basket when he was called away on an emergency. He promised to put up the hoop as soon as he returned. "No problem," I thought. "I have a brand new Spalding ball and a new cement drive on which to dribble it." For a few minutes I bounced the ball on the cement. Soon that became boring, so I took the ball and threw it up against the backboard—once. I let the ball run off the court and didn't pick it up until Dad returned to put up the rim. Why? It's no fun playing basketball without a goal. The joy is in having something to aim for.

That is the major difference between work and other enjoyable activities. Many times we find work is boring because there is no stated goal or purpose. We drag home tired, ready to sit down and relax. Then we remember, "Tonight is my bowling night." We go to the closet and pick up a sixteen-pound ball, get in the car and drive through traffic to throw that heavy ball down an alley for two hours! That doesn't make sense. We were tired and ready for rest, and now we are exercising (not working) harder than ever before. Why? All because there are ten pins at the end of the alley ... a tangible goal. Hitting them brings immediate reinforcements. The total motivation of bowling is the ten pins, the goal. If you don't believe that, just have the operator remove the pins. See how many times you will throw a sixteen-pound ball down the alley without them.

In order to have fun and direction in changing your attitudes, you must establish a clearly stated goal. This goal should be as specific as possible, written out and signed, with a time frame attached to it. The purpose statement should be placed in a visible spot where you see it several times a day to give you reinforcement. Here is an example of a statement of purpose:

"To change my attitude (specifically, negative thinking,

critical remarks toward others and resentment) by following the procedure outlined in Section IV of *Your Attitude: Key to Success*. To effectively accomplish this goal I will review this process and my progress daily by being accountable to an encouraging friend. By (time) _____ I fully expect that others will be noticing my positive behavior."

You will attain this goal if each day you do three things:

1. Write specifically what you desire to accomplish each day.

The story of David's encounter with Goliath is a fine illustration of faith and how it may move out against insurmountable odds with seemingly inadequate resources. But one thing perplexed me when I first began to study David's life. Why did he pick five stones for his sling on his way to encounter Goliath? I am convinced that the Scriptures never just use words for their own sake—the number of stones had to be significant. The longer I pondered the more perplexed I became. Why *five* stones? There was only one giant. Choosing five stones seemed to be a flaw in his faith. Did he think he was going to miss and that he would have four more chances? Some time later I was reading in 2 Samuel, and I got the answer. Goliath had four sons, so there were five giants. In David's reckoning, there was one stone per giant! Now this is what I mean about being specific in our faith.

What are the giants you must slay to make your attitude what it needs to be? What resources will you need? Don't be overcome with frustration when you see all the problems. Take one giant at a time. Military strategists teach their armies to fight on one front at a time. Settle which attitude you want to tackle at this time. Write it down. As you successfully begin to win battles, write them down. This will encourage you. Spend time reading about your past victories.

2. Verbalize to your encouraging friend what you want to accomplish each day.

Belief is inward conviction, faith is outward action. You will receive both encouragement and accountability by verbalizing your intentions. One of the ways people resolve a conflict is to verbalize it to themselves or someone else. This practice is also vital in reaching your desired attitudes.

I know successful salesmen who repeat this phrase out loud

fifty times each morning and fifty times each evening: "I can do it." Continually saying and hearing these positive statements helps them believe in themselves and causes them to act on that belief. Start this process by changing your vocabulary. Here are some suggestions:

ELIMINATE THESE WORDS COMPLETELY	MAKE THESE WORDS A PART OF YOUR VOCABULARY
1. I can't	1. I can
2. If	2. I will
3. Doubt	3. Expect the best
4. I don't think	4. I know
5. I don't have the time	5. I will make the time
6. Maybe	6. Positively
7. I'm afraid of	7. I am confident
8. I don't believe	8. I do believe
9. (minimize) I	9. (promote) You
10. It's impossible	10. God is able

3. Take action on what you write and verbalize what you wrote each day.

Jesus teaches us that the difference between a wise man and a foolish man is their response to what they already know. A wise man follows up on what he hears while a foolish man knows but does not act (Matthew 7:24-27).

We are told in James 1:22-25, "But prove yourself doers of the word, and not merely hearers who delude themselves. For if anyone is a hearer of the word and not a doer, he is like a man who looks at his natural face in a mirror; for once he has looked at himself and gone away, he has immediately forgotten what kind of a person he was. But one who looks intently at the perfect law, the law of liberty, and abides by it, not having become a forgetful hearer but an effectual doer, this man shall be blessed in what he does."

Action Suggestion: For thirty days, treat every person you meet as the most important person on earth. You will find that they will begin treating you the same way. How does the world look at you? Exactly how you look at the world. Do something positive for someone else regularly. No one is useless in this world who lightens the burden of it for someone else.

Choice #4—Have the desire to change.

No choice will determine the success of your attitude change more than desiring to change. When all else fails, desire alone can keep you heading in the right direction. Many people have climbed over insurmountable obstacles to make themselves better people when they realized that change is possible if you really want it bad enough. Let me illustrate.

While hopping about one day, a frog happened to slip into a very large pothole along a country road. All his attempts at jumping out were in vain. Soon a rabbit came upon the frog trapped in the hole and offered to help him out. He, too, failed. After various animals from the forest made three or four gallant attempts to help the poor frog out, they finally gave up. "We'll go back and get you some food," they said. "It looks like you're going to be there a while." However, not long after they took off to get food, they heard the frog hopping along after them. They couldn't believe it! "We thought you couldn't get out!" they exclaimed. "Oh, I couldn't," replied the frog. "But you see, there was a big truck coming right at me, and I had to."

It is when we "have to get out of the potholes of life" that we change. As long as we have acceptable options, we will not change. The person with too many options reminds me of a story two friends recently told me.

They have two nieces who are sisters. One is eleven years old and is an excellent swimmer. She spends a lot of time practicing for swim meets. The younger girl is five and also swims, but she shows no willingness to pay the price to practice and win in swim meets.

Over Christmas the older sister won a 220-meter race. Her father was reading the newspaper article about Lisa's success and asked the younger daughter, "Shelley, wouldn't you like to work hard and get your name in the paper and have a good time?" "Dad," she said, "I'd just rather sit here and eat cookies and drink milk the rest of my life."

Sadly, that's where too many people live. While they drink milk and eat cookies, others pay the price and win medals. Every once in a while the cookie eaters of life stop long enough to wonder why they don't have medals. A tinge of guilt might touch them for a moment, but then they decide to go back to "cookie dunking." They lack desire.

Most people are more comfortable with old problems than

new solutions. They respond to their need for a turn-around in life like the Duke of Cambridge, who once said, "Any change, at any time, for any reason is to be deplored." People who believe that nothing should ever be done for the first time never see anything done.

Cotford's Law states, "Nothing is ever done until everyone is convinced that it ought to be done and has been convinced for so long that it is now time to do something else."

But there is hope. There seem to be three times in our lives when we're most receptive to change. First, when we hurt so much that we are forced to change. Jesus tells about this type of individual in Luke 15. The parable of the prodigal son illustrates that when we are looking up from the bottom of a fifteen-foot pit it is possible to "come to ourselves" and get help by going back to father's house.

The prodigal acted similarly to the lady with an incurable disease who came to Jesus only after she had "spent all that she had" (Luke 8:43) on other doctors and had become desperate.

For more than a year I taught Bible studies on miracles. At the end of this series I wrote down a few basic truths about this subject. My greatest discovery was that every miracle in the Bible began with a problem. Only when someone was hurting did they receive relief. Only when a person was questioning did they find answers. Now this truth has bad news and good news in it. The bad news is that usually our hurt has to be great enough to create a desire to change. We only gain after pain. The good news is that if you are desperate and need to change, you are a candidate for a miracle.

Receptivity to change is also heightened, second, when we are bored and become restless. Everyone experiences this at certain times in his life. Perhaps the wife senses this when the children are all in school and she finds extra time to get involved with other things. Husbands plateau on their jobs and begin to lose interest in their work. A holy dissatisfaction can be healthy when it produces positive changes.

It is a sad day for any person when he becomes so satisfied with his life, his thoughts and his deeds, that he ceases to be challenged to do greater things in life.

Third, change is apt to occur when we realize we *can* change.

This is the greatest motivation of all. Nothing sparks the fires of desire more than the sudden realization that you do not have to stay the same. You no longer need to feel the burden of negative attitudes. You have no valid reason to constantly feel bitter and resentful about life, others or yourself. You can change!

Because I firmly believe that people will change once they understand it is possible, I continually share one phrase with others. When I sense bewilderment, doubt, frustration and other mental blocks, I say, "Yes you can." I have seen hundreds of faces light up with those three simple words and an encouraging smile.

A few weeks ago, my wife and I stopped at a fast food restaurant to buy some soft drinks. When I asked for a diet cola for Margaret, the young lady said they had no diet drinks. Then I asked her for a large cup of ice, thinking that I could stop at a market down the road and buy a can of diet soda. My request created a cloud on my waitress' face as she said, "Sir, I don't think we can do that here." "Yes you can," I replied quickly and confidently. Immediately her face lit up and she responded enthusiastically. She went off to get my cup of ice. All she needed was someone to help her believe she could do what she'd been asked.

My life is dedicated to helping others reach their potential. I suggest that you follow the advice of Mark Twain, who said, "Take your mind out every now and then and dance on it. It is getting all caked up." It was his way of saying, "Get out of that rut." Too many times we settle into a set way of thinking and accept limitations that need not be placed upon us.

Life is a changing process. With all of its transitions come new opportunities for growth. What is a limiting factor yesterday may not be one today. Accept the following statement for your life: "The days ahead are filled with changes which are my challenges. I will respond to these opportunities with the confidence that my life will be better because of them. With God all things are possible."

Desire increases with love. Fall in love with the challenge of change and watch the desire to change grow. We have all known a desire that can only be expressed in the words, "Love made me do it."

Aleida Huissen, 78, of Rotterdam, Netherlands, had been

smoking for fifty years. For fifty years she tried to give up the habit, but was unsuccessful. Then last year, Leo Jensen, 79, proposed marriage and refused to go through with the wedding until Aleida gave up smoking. Aleida says, "Will power never was enough to get me off the habit. Love did it."

Be careful what you set your heart on!

Luther Burbank fell in love with plants.
Edison fell in love with invention.
Ford fell in love with motor cars.
Kettering fell in love with research.
The Wright brothers fell in love with airplanes.

Be very careful what you set your heart on, for it will surely come true!

"Delight yourself in the Lord and He will give you the desires of your heart" (Psalm 37:4).

Choice #5—Live one day at a time.

Any man can fight the battle for just one day. It is only when you and I add the burdens of those two awful eternities, yesterday and tomorrow, that we tremble. It is not the experiences of today that drive men to distraction; it is the remorse or bitterness for something that happened yesterday and the dread of what tomorrow may bring. Let us therefore live but one day at a time—today!

David, in his prayer for forgiveness (Psalm 51), asked God to "Hide Thy face from my sins." He understood that effectiveness today is determined by the healing and forgetting of yesterday. "My sin is ever before me," describes a condition in David's life that would have hindered the change he wanted to make. Therefore he used words that pointedly asked God to spiritually heal his mind and heart. "Blot out my transgressions ... wash me thoroughly ... cleanse me from my sin ... purify me ... wash me ... make me to hear joy and gladness ... blot out all my iniquities ... create in me a clean heart ... renew a steadfast spirit within me ... restore to me the joy of my salvation ... deliver me."

Like David, you should pray these phrases and allow God to forgive you and heal your past. Only God can heal what happened yesterday and help you live effectively today. What you have not overcome in your past remains to plague you in your present.

Yesterday I met an old friend at a conference. While I spoke, I noticed a new joy upon his face. During one of the breaks he came up and gave me a big hug. "John," he said, "recently during a prayer time God healed me of the scars in my past." This man had undergone severe negative experiences and now was sensing a freedom and power to live today. Now, after you have been assured of forgiveness from God, it is important to concentrate on building a new you.

Choice #6—Change your thought patterns.

That which holds our attention, determines our actions. We are where we are and what we are because of the dominating thoughts that occupy our minds. William James said, "The greatest discovery of my generation is that people can alter their lives by altering their attitudes of mind." Romans 12:1,2 says, "I urge you therefore, brethren, by the mercies of God, to present your bodies a living and holy sacrifice, acceptable to God, which is your spiritual service of worship. And do not be conformed to this world, but be transformed by the renewing of your mind, that you may prove what the will of God is, that which is good and acceptable and perfect."

Two things must be stated to emphasize the power of our thought life. Major premise: We can control our thoughts. Minor premise: Our feelings come from our thoughts. Conclusion? We can control our feelings by learning to change one thing: The way we think. It is that simple. Our feelings come from our thoughts. Therefore, we can change them by changing our thought patterns.

Our thought life, not our circumstances, determines our happiness. Often I see people who are convinced that they will be happy when they attain a certain goal. When they reach the goal, many times they do not find the fulfillment they anticipated.

You often can see this phenomenon among mothers. First they say, "When Johnny gets out of elementary school, I'll be happy!" And they are, for a while. Next you hear them telling their friends, "When Johnny graduates from high school, I'll be so happy!" And they are, at least for the summer. Johnny's graduation from college brings the same result, and so does Johnny's marriage. So does the birth of Johnny's first child, when Momma becomes an ecstatic grandmother, and the feeling may continue until she becomes a baby-sitter.

But if Momma has not learned how to be happy between her special blessings, she will not have a steady, enjoyable life.

The secret to staying on an even keel? Fill your mind with "whatever is true, whatever is honorable, whatever is right, whatever is pure, whatever is lovely, whatever is of good repute, if there is any excellence and if anything is worthy of praise, let your mind dwell on these things" (Philippians 4:8). Paul understood. That which holds our attention determines our action.

Choice #7—Develop good habits.

Attitudes are nothing more than habits of thought. Here is a cycle that will help you form proper habits:

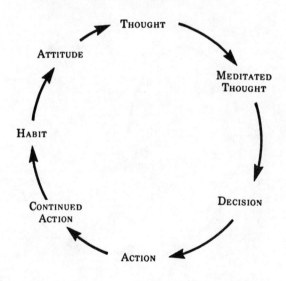

This cycle can be positive or negative. The process for developing habits, good or bad, is the same. It is as easy to form a habit of succeeding as it is to succumb to the habit of failure. Observe the next two cycles and see the difference.

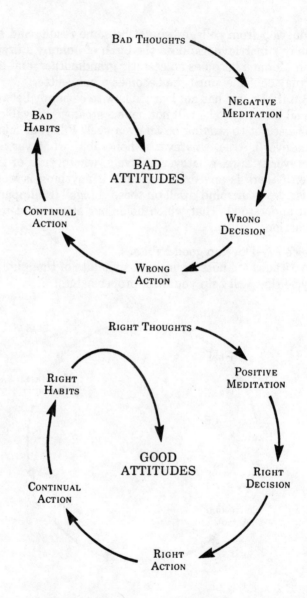

Habits aren't instincts; they're acquired actions or reactions. They don't just happen, they are caused. Once the original cause of a habit is determined, it is within your power to accept or reject it. Most people allow their habits to control them. When those habits are hurtful, they damage our attitudes. The following formula will assist you in changing bad habits into good ones.

STEP #1—List your bad habits.
STEP #2—What was the original cause?
STEP #3—What are the supporting causes?
STEP #4—Determine a positive habit to replace the bad one.
STEP #5—Think about the good habit, its benefits and results.
STEP #6—Take action to develop this habit.
STEP #7—Daily act upon this habit for reinforcement.
STEP #8—Reward yourself by noting one of the benefits from your good habit.

Choice #8—Continually choose to have a right attitude.

Once you make the choice to possess a good attitude the work really begins. Now comes a life of continual deciding to grow and maintaining the right outlook. Attitudes have a tendency to revert back to their original pattterns if not carefully guarded and cultivated.

"The hardest thing about milking cows," observed a farmer, "is that they never stay milked." Attitudes often don't stay changed. There are three stages of change in which you must deliberately choose the right attitude.

Early Stage—The first few days are always the most difficult. Old habits are hard to break. The mental process must be on guard continually to provide right action.

Middle Stage—The moment good habits begin to take root, options open that bring on new challenges. New habits are formed that will either be good or bad. The good news is: "Like begets like." The more right choices and habits you develop, the more likely good habits will be formed.

Later Stage—Complacency can become the enemy. We all know of incidents where someone (perhaps us) successfully lost weight, only to fall back into old eating habits and gain it back.

Our decision to continually choose the right attitude will bring many benefits. A friend with whom I have worked for five years on attitude change, recently told a large conference of leaders, "If you knew me five years ago, you would not recognize me today. My family, ministry and self-image have greatly improved. Daily I work on my attitudes. I am not what I want to be, but I'm not what I used to be either. I want to grow in the next five years like I have the last five. To do this I must continually choose the right attitude." There is no improvement except through change. To improve continually we must change continually.

You are the key to changing your attitude. When faced with the need for improvement, too many people are like the man who walked into a psychiatrist's office. He had placed half a cantaloupe on his head for a hat. Around each ear he had wrapped a piece of bacon. The psychiatrist rubbed his hands in glee, "I've got a live one this time," he thought to himself. Then the man with the cantaloupe on his head and pieces of bacon wrapped around each ear sat down. "I've come," he said to the psychiatrist, "to talk to you about my brother."

No one but you can determine what you will think and how you will act. That is good! Now, take control and begin the exciting journey of attitude improvement.

IT'S UP TO YOU!

If you think you're a winner you'll win,
If you dare to step out you'll succeed.
Believe in your heart, have a purpose to start.
Aim to help fellow man in his need.

Thoughts of faith must replace every doubt.
Words of courage and you cannot fail.
If you stumble and fall, rise and stand ten feet tall,
You determine the course that you sail.

For in life as in death don't you see,
It's the man who has nothing to fear,
Who approaches the gates, stands for a moment and waits,
Feels the presence of God oh so near.

You've been given the power to see,
What it takes to be a real man,
Let your thinking be pure, it will make you secure.
If you want to, you know that you can.

—Author unknown

13

THE OPPORTUNITIES AROUND YOU

"There are two keys that determine who we are: who we conceive ourselves to be and who we associate with."

—John Maxwell

ONCE YOU HAVE MADE the choice to change your attitude, you are ready to allow the "opportunities around you" to make this decision a success.

Opportunity #1—Enlist the cooperation of a friend.

Deuteronomy 32:30, "How could one chase a thousand, and two put ten thousand to flight, unless their Rock had sold them, and the Lord had given them up?"

We need each other! Few people are successful unless a lot of people want them to be. Change has a tendency to intimidate us. Add to that intimidation the realization that we have a long way to go before proper attitudes are established and we begin to feel like the two cows grazing in a pasture who saw a milk truck pass. On the side of the truck were the words, "Pasteurized, homogenized, standardized, Vitamin A added." One cow sighed and said to the other, "Makes you feel sort of inadequate, doesn't it?"

To help you overcome this feeling of inadequacy, you need the help of a friend. Find someone who has the spirit of Tanzing, the native guide of Edmund Hillary, who made the historic climb of Mt. Everest.

Coming down from the peak, Hillary suddenly lost his footing. Tanzing held the line taut and kept them both from falling by digging his ax into the ice. Later Tanzing refused any special credit for saving Hillary's life; he considered it a routine part of the job. As he put it, "Mountain climbers always help each other."

Tanzing realized that we can never do anything for others that will not have some eventual benefits for ourselves. There is a law of life which will, in time, return good for good. Therefore, enlisting someone's help will not only assist you, but it will also give a friend a blessing in return.

Conditions needed for successful cooperative effort:

1. A friend you can see or talk to daily.
2. Someone who loves you and is an encourager.
3. Someone with whom you have mutual honesty and transparency.
4. A person who is successful in overcoming problems.
5. Someone who has strong faith in God and believes in miracles.

The book of Acts opens with the excitement of the early church. In the midst of all the joy and growth we see a very significant situation—John and Peter together in ministry and fellowship. The reason? John was encouraging Peter. A few weeks previously, Peter had denied his Lord and wasn't doing particularly well. In fact, he wanted to return to fishing. John, the disciple of love, decided to make Peter his ministry. Acts 3 records the miraculous healing of the lame man, but there was another healing taking place in Peter's life, an inner healing, as John walked with him to the Temple. Could it be that Peter's greatness was at least partially a result of John's acceptance? Go find a friend like John.

Opportunity #2—Associate with the right people.

One morning I walked into my office and saw the following note on top of my desk: "Good morning, Pastor Maxwell, there are two keys that determine who we are: (1) who we perceive ourselves to be and (2) who we associate with."

How true. Yet, as I reflect on that note I conclude that a large portion of our self-image (who we conceive ourselves to be) is determined by our friendships. Accepting attitudes are based many times on how important the attitude is in complementing or damaging the image we feel other people have of us.

Birds of a feather do flock together. From friends we acquire many of our thoughts, mannerisms and characteristics. Changing an attitude from negative to positive often requires changing friendships. It is no accident that kids with good grades run around with other kids with good grades. While counseling people facing a broken marriage, I have observed that often the couple's friends are having marriage problems.

Many times I listen to people blame circumstances for their problems. But usually it is the crowd we run with, not the circumstances we encounter, that makes the difference in our lives. Good circumstances with bad friends result in defeat. Bad circumstances with good friends result in victory.

Some time ago I was listening to commentator Paul Harvey on the radio. He opened the show with the true story of a couple who had applied to adopt a young girl. The couple was turned down by the agency, not because of debt or personality conflicts, but because, according to the agency, their "attitude was too good." They argued that the girl would not get a realistic view of today's world, a view of both the bad and the good side of life.

Can you believe that? I hope you will associate with friends who are positive and keep you from a "realistic" view of today's world. Although it is unrealistic to surround yourself with only positive people, it is possible to choose friends that have a proper outlook on life.

Opportunity #3—Select a model to follow.

Communicators say that ninety percent of what we learn is visual, nine percent is audio and one percent comes through the other senses. Our dependence on the eyes to learn, no doubt, is at least partially a result of television in our culture. Visual messages last longer than those we just hear. The ideal combination for learning is to see and hear. You could select someone to follow who would give you a constant visualization of what you want to become. Making a single decision to alter an attitude is not enough. The vision of what you desire must be constantly before you. To achieve the kind of life you want, you must act, walk, talk and conduct yourself as the ideal person that you visualize yourself to be. Gradually that old self will pass away and be replaced with the new one.

The apostle Paul understood and practiced the importance of modeling. In almost every letter to the churches he encouraged the people to follow his example. He told the church at Philippi, "The things you have learned and received and heard and seen in me, practice these things; and the God of peace shall be with you" (Philippians 4:9). He reminded Timothy, when encouraging him to be an overcomer, "You followed my teaching, conduct, purpose, faith, love, perseverance, persecutions and sufferings . . . " (2 Timothy 4:10,11). Peter commands spiritual leaders "to be examples of the flock" (1 Peter 5:3). The greatest of motivational principles is: "People do what people see." As adults we are still playing follow the leader. Nothing will more effectively inspire you to change than having a beautiful example to follow.

My attitudes came as a result of proper modeling by my parents. Usually while speaking at conferences and trying to help people with their attitudes, I give several illustrations from my home life. One couple who listened to these illustrations desperately wanted to change themselves and their children. They decided to invite Mom and Dad into their home for a weekend. This time spent together was helpful. One day while my mother was gone, the hostess entered the guest room and began to pray, and she asked God to give her my mother's wisdom and positive strengths just as Elijah's mantle had fallen on the prophet Elisha.

In 1981 I visited the Santiago Methodist Pentecostal Church in Chile, South America. The congregation numbered more than 85,000 members. My heart was moved as I witnessed the wonderful work that God was doing through that congregation. Within a month I would become the senior pastor at Skyline Wesleyan Church in San Diego, California. My desire was to build a great church for God. Realizing that Pastor Vasquez had been greatly blessed by the Lord, I asked him to lay hands upon me and pray for God's anointing on my ministry. I look back on that incident and rejoice that I had a model to follow, if only for a few days.

Begin looking for someone to stretch your life. If no one seems to be available, ask God to send you a Christian with a winning attitude. Ask that individual to disciple you for a few months. Enjoy the experience of growth by example.

Opportunity #4—Learn from your mistakes.

Pace-setters' Prayer: "Lord, give me the courage to fail; for if I have failed, at least I have tried. Amen."

The first instant an idea is conceived is a moment of decision. When an opportunity for growth is opened to you, what do you tell yourself? Will you grasp the chance with a tingle of excitement and say, "I can make it work!" or do you smother it by saying, "That's impractical ... too difficult ... I don't think it can be done"? In that moment, you choose between success and failure. You help to form a habit of either positive or negative thinking by what you tell yourself! So give your "better" self a chance to grow. Form the habit of positive reaction followed by positive action. We cannot cause the wind to blow the way we want, but we can adjust our sails so that they will take us where we want to go.

You cannot control all circumstances. You cannot always make right decisions which bring right results. But you can always learn from your mistakes. The following formula will assist you in this process.

Formula for overcoming failure:

1. Recognize

What is failure? Is it permanent? Is there a second chance? Complete this sentence by circling the right phrase.

A person is a failure when
(a) he makes a mistake;
(b) he quits;
(c) someone thinks he is.

2. Review

Failure should be our teacher, not our undertaker. Failure is delay, not defeat. It is a temporary detour, not a dead-end street. A winner is big enough to admit his mistakes, smart enough to profit from them and strong enough to correct them. The only difference between the unsuccessful man and the successful man is that the unsuccessful man is mistaken three times out of five while the successful man is right three times out of five.

3. Repress

Perhaps your own personal problems and hang-ups cause the failure. If so, begin to work immediately on self-discipline. If you are the problem, put yourself under control. Lord Nelson, England's famous naval hero, suffered from seasickness

137

throughout his entire life. Yet the man who had destroyed Napoleon's fleet did not let illness interfere with his career. He not only learned to live with his personal weakness, but he also conquered it. Most of us have our own little seasickness, too. For some it may be physical, for others psychological. Usually it is a private war carried on quietly within us. No one will pin a medal on us for winning it, but nothing can dim the satisfaction of knowing that we did not surrender.

4. Readjust

An eminent plastic surgeon told of a boy who lost his hand at the wrist. When he asked the lad about his handicap, the boy replied, "I don't have a handicap, sir. I just don't have a right hand." Dr. Brown went on to discover that this boy was one of the leading scorers on his high school football team. It's not what you have lost, but what you have left that counts.

5. Re-enter

Mistakes mark the road to success. He who makes no mistakes makes no progress. Make sure you generate a reasonable number of mistakes. I know that comes naturally to some people, but too many people are so afraid of error that they make their lives rigid with checks and counterchecks, discourage change and, in the end, so structure themselves that they will miss the kind of offbeat opportunity that can send their life skyrocketing. So take a look at your record, and if you come to the end of a year and see that you haven't made many mistakes, ask yourself if you have tried everything you should have.

It is a cliche to say that we learn by our mistakes, but I'll state the case more strongly than that. I'll say you can't learn without mistakes. One reason some people never grow through change is that they can't stand failure. Even the best people have a lot more failures than success. The secret is that they don't let the failures upset them. They do their very best. Let the chips fall where they may, then go on to the next attempt.

In big league baseball, anyone who gets three or more hits in ten trips to the plate is a superstar. It's a matter of percentages. And in life, it's the same way. When you strike out, forget it. If you made some mistakes, learn from them and do better the next time. Strikeouts are part of the game, nothing to be ashamed of. Just get in there and keep swinging!

Opportunity #5—Expose yourself to successful experiences.

It takes five positive experiences to overcome one negative situation. When faced with the possibility of failure, our tendency is to sit back and be anxious. Fear is nature's warning signal to get busy. We overcome it by successful action.

I once heard a speaker say, "We overcome by action." That is only partially true. Experiences that are continually unsuccessful can increase our desire to sit out the game in the arena of life. Action that produces confidence and a degree of success will encourage us to attempt new challenges.

I learned this when I played basketball in my high school. One year our coach had a "brilliant" idea that would help us shoot our foul shots with greater accuracy. He replaced the regulation basketball rim with one that was smaller. He thought that if we could hit the smaller basket, it would be a cinch for us to make the larger one in the game. I watched my teammates practice foul shooting on the smaller rim. They missed frequently and seemed frustrated. Since I was captain of the team and an 80 percent shot from the foul line, I decided to approach my coach cautiously. My theory was opposite his. It was my belief that continually missing foul shots on the smaller rim would create an image of failure and result in missed shots in a game. That was exactly the result! Thinking back on that incident makes me wonder what would have happened if the coach had placed larger rims upon the backboard.

Nothing intimidates us more than constant exposure to failure. Nothing motivates us more than constant exposure to success. Therefore, I have found that people change more quickly if they are continually given situations in which they can be successful. Believing this, I set out to teach my daughter Elizabeth how to hit a ball with the bat. I didn't want her to stop swinging just because she might miss, because that would have given her a sense of failure, so I gave her the following instructions. "Elizabeth, it is your responsibility to swing the bat. It is my job to hit the bat with the ball when I pitch it."

139

Elizabeth fearlessly began to swing the bat. She had nothing to lose! Every time she would swing the bat she was a success. The problem—I kept missing the bat with the ball I was throwing. Finally, after many swings and as many misses, Elizabeth threw down the bat, looked at me with disgust and said, "Daddy, you keep missing the bat!"

Start exposing yourself today to successful people and experiences. Read books that will make you a better person. Find something that you can do well and do it often. Help make someone who needs your spiritual gifts a better person. Feed your right attitudes, and before you know it your bad ones will starve to death. Write down your success and review them often. Share your growth with those who are interested in you and already have excellent attitudes. Take time daily to congratulate yourself and thank others for making this change of attitude possible.

14

THE GOD ABOVE YOU

"When I am secure in Christ, I can afford to take a risk in my life. Only the insecure cannot afford to risk failure. The secure can be honest about themselves. They can admit failure. They are able to seek help and try again. They can change."
—*John Maxwell*

"A DISTINGUISHED FOREIGNER was a big help to the American colonists during the Revolutionary War," the history teacher said. "Can you give me his name, Tommy?"

"God," Tommy answered.

E. Stanley Jones made an impressive point when he said, "Anything less than God will let you down." And he went on to explain, "Anything less than God is not rooted in eternal reality. It has a built-in failure." For every possible predicament of man, there is a corresponding grace of God. In other words: For every particular human need there is a particular supernatural resource. For every definite problem there is a definite answer. For every hurt there is a cure. For every weakness there is a strength. For every confusion there is guidance.

If you can understand that truth your life can be different. Jeremiah understood it when he said, "Ah Lord God! Behold, Thou hast made the heavens and the earth by Thy great power and by Thine outstretched arm! Nothing is too difficult for Thee" (32:17). One of my favorite verses is in 2 Chronicles 16:9. "For the eyes of the Lord move to and fro throughout the earth that He may strongly support those whose heart is completely His."

There are several ways that God supports and strengthens our lives while we change.

Strength #1—God's Word

When the truths of the Bible permeate our mind and heart, our attitude can only improve. His Word is filled with people who continually demonstrate that man's right relationship with God gives him a healthy mind-set. Paul is just one example.

"I wonder why it is," an Anglican bishop once pondered, "that everywhere the apostle Paul went they had a revolution, and everywhere I go they serve a cup of tea."

Today we live relatively easy lives. But the Apostle Paul could hardly set foot in a city before a riot started. It seemed like Paul was always getting into trouble! During his first missionary journey he was stoned and left for dead. During his second missionary journey he eluded arrest on charges of turning the world upside down. Throughout his life Paul experienced incredible hardships: imprisonment, flogging, beatings, lashings, shipwreck, destitution, exhaustion. Hardly the "victorious Christian life" we often visualize, wouldn't you say? But despite his intense hardships and sufferings, Paul consistently maintained an attitude of thankfulness and joy. They threw him in a prison: What did he do? Grumble and complain? No! He sang hymns of joy to God (Acts 16:25). They threw him into prison again. He encouraged others to "rejoice in the Lord always" (Philippians 4:4). Paul's dominant attitude—whatever his circumstance—was joy. Where did Paul's joy come from?

Perhaps we can gain insight into Paul's victorious life by reading his letter to the Romans. Chapter 8 gives us what I call, Belief Foundations for a Positive Christian Attitude.

First Foundation—"I am truly significant."

"And we know that God causes all things to work together for good to those who love God, to those who are called according to His purpose. For whom He foreknew, He also predestined to become conformed to the image of His Son, that He might be the first-born among many brethren; and whom He predestined, these He also called; and whom He called, these He also justified; and whom He justified, these He also glorified" (vs. 28-30).

My sense of significance grows upon realizing that I am "called according to His purpose" (v. 28); "predestined to become conformed to the image of His Son" (v. 29); "called ... justified ... glorified" (v. 30).

Second Foundation—"I am truly secure."

"What then shall we say to these things? If God is for us, who is against us? He who did not spare His own Son, but delivered Him up for us all, how will He not also with Him freely give us all things? Who will bring a charge against God's elect? God is the one who justifies; who is the one who condemns? Christ Jesus is He who died, yes, rather who was raised, who is at the right hand of God, who also intercedes for us. Who shall separate us from the love of Christ? Shall tribulation, or distress, or persecution, or famine, or nakedness, or peril, or sword? Just as it is written, 'For Thy sake we are being put to death all day long; we were considered as sheep to be slaughtered.' But in all these things we overwhelmingly conquer through Him who loved us. For I am convinced that neither death, nor life, nor angels, nor principalities, nor things present, nor things to come, nor powers, nor height, nor depth, nor any other created thing shall be able to separate us from the love of God, which is in Christ Jesus our Lord" (vs. 31-39).

When I know that I am secure in Him, I can afford to take a risk in my life. Only the insecure cannot afford to risk failure. The secure can be honest about themselves. They can admit failure. They are able to seek help and try again. They can change.

Many times people ask me to help them overcome some deep problems of their past. One person was having an especially difficult time letting go of his past. This individual's background was horrible—broken home, suicide, failure in business, mental problems and no love. Then, in desperation, there was a desire for a new life, a healing of the mind as well as the soul. That day I shared a scripture that will also encourage you.

"Do not call to mind the former things, or ponder things of the past. Behold, I do something new, now it will spring forth; will you not be aware of it? I will even make a roadway in the wilderness, rivers in the desert" (Isaiah 43:18,19).

Remember the words of Jeremiah, "Is anything too hard for the Lord?" The Bible, not Norman Vincent Peale, first said,

"All things are possible to him who believes." God's Word, not Maxwell Maltz, author of *Psycho-Cybernetics*, first said, "All things for which you pray and ask, believe that you have received them, and they shall be granted you." The Scriptures, not Robert L. Schuller, first said, "Everything you ask in prayer, believing, you shall receive." God's Word gives us encouragement and guidance to change our lives.

Strength #2—Prayer

Psalm 25:1-10 is a short, simple and sincere prayer. Yet, it is also successful. Many outstanding prayers in the Bible were effective yet brief. The Lord's Prayer consists of 56 words. Compare that with the 26,911 words in a recent government order setting the price of cabbage.

Recently I read in the Colorado Legal Secretaries Association Newsletter that if an attorney had written the first line of the Lord's Prayer, "Give us this day our daily bread," it might have read like this: "We respectfully petition, request and entreat that due and adequate provision be made, this date and date first above inscribed, for satisfying of petitioner's nutritional requirements and for the organizing of such methods of allocation and distribution as may be deemed necessary and proper to assure the reception by and for said petitioners of such quantity of cereal products (hereinafter called "bread") as shall, in the judgment of the afore, and petitioners, constitute sufficient amount."

Psalm 25 describes a person who has chosen the right road, yet has not found it always easy to walk. The path is lined with enemies who would like nothing better than to put the weaker to shame. The traveler is also plagued with internal doubts as he recalls previous wanderings and failures. What he must realize is that the road is too difficult to walk without the companionship and friendship of God. The psalmist, troubled from without and within, has stopped for a moment in the way. He knows he cannot turn back, but scarcely knows how to continue. Therefore, he prays that God will help him follow through on his decision to stay on the right road.

We learn five things from this man of prayer in Psalm 25:1-10.

1. He knows in which direction to look for help.

"To Thee, O Lord, I lift up my soul" (v. 1). The humanist looks only to available human resources. The Christian immediately looks to God. The praying man realizes that God's blessings are not optional, they are a necessity.

2. He knows in whom to trust.

"O my God, in Thee I trust, do not let me be ashamed; do not let my enemies exalt over me. Indeed, none of those who wait for Thee will be ashamed; those who deal treacherously without cause will be ashamed" (vs. 2,3).

An attitude of trust is the key to effective praying based on the character of God. The thrust of our trust must be Godward.

3. He knows the purpose of prayer.

"Make me know Thy ways, O Lord; teach me Thy paths. Lead me in Thy truth and teach me. For Thou art the God of my salvation; for Thee I wait all the day" (vs. 4,5).

The purpose of prayer is to change. Richard Foster says, "To pray is to change. Prayer is the central avenue God uses to transform us. If we are unwilling to change, we will abandon prayer as a noticeable characteristic of our lives. The more we pray, the more we come to the heartbeat of God. Prayer starts the communication process between ourselves and God. All the options of life fall before us. At that point we will either forsake our prayer life and cease to grow, or we will pursue our prayer life and let Him change us. Either option is painful. To not grow in His likeness is to not enjoy His fullness. When this happens, a haunting voice continues to ask, 'What could I have become in Him if I would have been a man of prayer?' To grow in His likeness is to enjoy His fullness. When this happens, the priorities of the world begin to fade away." When we pray asking God to change a situation, He usually begins with us.

4. He knows the basis of prayer.

"Remember, O Lord, Thy compassion and Thy lovingkindness, for they have been from of old. Do not remember the sins of my youth or my transgressions; according to Thy lovingkindness remember Thou me, for Thy goodness' sake, O Lord" (vs. 6,7).

The Psalmist cannot approach God on the basis of his own greatness so he comes, "according to Thy lovingkindness." David's change is based on who God is, not what He does.

5. He knows the future of prayer.

"Good and upright is the Lord: therefore He instructs sinners in the way. He leads the humble in justice, and He teaches the humble His way. All the paths of the Lord are lovingkindness and truth to those who keep His covenant and His testimonies" (vs. 8-10).

The future is as solid as God's character. The faithfulness of God is based on His attributes, not your actions. Take those wrong attitudes to Him. Pray the prayer of Psalm 24:4-5.

Make me—Bring my attitudes under Your control
    (implies trials).

Teach me—Prepare me to know Your truth (implies teachings).

Lead me—Guide and walk with me in it (implies trust).
    This order keeps us from wandering off the path.

Lead me—cannot come first.
    We cannot trust what we do not know.
    We cannot trust what we have not tried.

Teach me—cannot come first.
    Learning without discipline (make me) cannot be fully
      effective.
    Learning without experience (lead me) cannot be fully
      appreciated.

Make me—must come first.
    Once the will is settled, the way is secure.
    Once the price is paid, the pathway is plain.

Prayer changes you. You change your attitudes.

Strength #3—The Holy Spirit

In the New Testament the Spirit is referred to nearly 300 times. The one word with which He is constantly associated is "power." Jesus in John 16:4-16 teaches clearly the need for the Helper in our lives. The disciples were insecure about their future. Jesus said, "But these things I have spoken to you, that when their hour comes, you may remember that I told you of them. And these things I did not say to you at the beginning, because I was with you. But now I am going to Him who sent Me; and none of you asks Me, 'Where are You going?' But because I have said these things to you, sorrow has filled your heart. But I tell you the truth, it is to your advantage that I go away; for if I do not go away, the Helper shall not come to you; but if I go, I will send Him to you. and He, when He comes, will convict the world concerning sin, and righteousness, and judgment; concerning sin, because they do not believe in Me; and concerning righteousness, because I go to the Father, and you no longer behold Me; and concerning judgment, because the ruler of this world has been judged. I have many more things to say to you, but you cannot hear them now. But when He, the Spirit of truth, comes, He will guide you into all the truth; for He will not speak on His own initiative, but whatever He hears, He will speak; and He will disclose to you what is to come. He shall glorify Me; for He shall take of Mine, and shall disclose it to you. All things that the Father has are Mine; therefore I said, that He takes of Mine, and will disclose it to you. A little while, and you will no longer behold Me; and again a little while, and you will see Me."

Jesus said it was "to our advantage" that He would leave so the "Helper" could be sent to us. "The Spirit of truth" will guide us and glorify Jesus. In Acts 1 we read that our Lord was ready to go back to the Father. Surrounded by a few followers, Jesus shared with them these last important words, in Acts 1:4-8, "He commanded them not to leave Jerusalem, but to wait for what the Father had promised, 'Which,' He said, 'you heard of from Me; for John baptized with water, but you shall be baptized with the Holy Spirit not many days from now.' And so when they had come together, they were asking Him, saying, 'Lord, is it at this time You are restoring the Kingdom to Israel?' He said to them, 'It is not for you to know times or epochs which the Father has fixed by His own authority; but you shall receive power when the Holy Spirit has come upon you; and you shall be My witnesses both in Jerusalem, and in all Judea and Samaria, and even to the remotest part of the earth.''

Power was promised when the Holy Spirit was received. Until Pentecost, the disciples were at best a questionable crew. Of the original twelve, Judas was already gone. James and John certainly were to be questioned over their motives and political desires. Thomas, from Missouri no doubt, continually doubted. (He was probably the father of the church board member.) And there is Peter—glorious one moment, gone the next. Declaring truths, then denying them. What were his plans after the death of Christ? He had fishing on his mind.

Jesus had spent three years with the disciples. They had listened to His teaching, yet they needed something more than learning. He had performed many miracles, yet they were frustrated with their inadequate human endeavors. Upon the disciples' request, Jesus taught them to pray, yet they lacked real power in their lives. The Lord's discipline still had not given his small group of followers the effectiveness they needed to begin the early church. Jesus knew what they needed. Therefore, He encouraged them to wait for the filling of the Holy Spirit in their lives.

They waited, and they were filled. The early church was launched! The theme of this growing group of believers was "forward through storm." Seven difficult problems confronted this New Testament Church of the book of Acts. After each obstacle, we read that the church was enlarged and the Word of God multiplied. Setbacks became springboards. Obstacles were turned into opportunities. Barriers turned out to be blessings. Cowards became courageous. Why? Those within the church were filled with the Holy Spirit.

That same power can be given to you. Changing an attitude is never easy. I have witnessed many attitudes make a positive turnaround through prayer. The following is the case study of a man we will call Jim. He is 33 years old, had a legalistic background, experienced physical abuse as a child (spankings, constant slappings, excessive religious standards, poor father-son relationship, low self-esteem). Jim says, "We were living in perpetual guilt. Early conversion to Christ was motivated by guilt. If something was fun, then it had to be sin. At age 15, I deserted God and ran away from home. When I returned, I did have a genuine experience of salvation. However, it was more than two years before I began to see a light at the end of the tunnel for my rotten attitude. It was during class at Bible College when the Holy Spirit spoke to my heart. I raised my hand and was recognized. I said, 'Professor, would you pray for me? My attitude stinks.' The entire class prayed for me and I experienced an immediate deliverance. My attitude has slipped from time to time, but I have noticed (and so have those around me) a constant improvement since. I still need improvement, but I'm doing better. Praise the Lord."

As you desire to change and act on your plans to change, remember you're not doing this by yourself; 1 John 4:4 says: "You are from God, little children, and have overcome them, because greater is He who is in you than he who is in the world."

YOU WILL EXPERIENCE THAT OVERCOMING POWER AS YOU REMEMBER THIS:

FORMULA FOR SPIRITUAL SUCCESS

If you want to be distressed—look within.
If you want to be defeated—look back.
If you want to be distracted—look around.
If you want to be dismayed—look ahead.
If you want to be delivered—look up!

CHART FOR CHANGE

Daily review this chart. It is designed to
1. encourage you in your pursuit of change;
2. direct you so you won't lose momentum; and
3. fill you with the right information.
Remember: There is no improvement except through change!

CHANNELS FOR CHANGE
I—THE CHOICE WITHIN YOU:

CHOICE #1—EVALUATE YOUR PRESENT ATTITUDES (Philippians 2:5). Are my attitudes today pleasing Christ and me?

CHOICE #2—THINK, IS YOUR FAITH STRONGER THAN FEAR (Matthew 21:21)? Am I taking faith-action on my present fears?

CHOICE #3—WRITE A STATEMENT OF PURPOSE (Philippians 3:13-14). Have I written, verbalized and acted on a plan to change my attitude?

CHOICE #4—DETERMINE IF YOU HAVE THE DESIRE TO CHANGE (Psalm 37:4). Change is possible *if* I want it bad enough. Am I willing to pay the price?

CHOICE #5—LIVE ONE DAY AT A TIME (Matthew 6:34). Am I allowing tomorrow's troubles to sap me of today's strength?

CHOICE #6—CHANGE YOUR THOUGHT PATTERNS (Philippians 4:8). That which holds our attention determines our action. Am I thinking on the right things?

CHOICE #7—DEVELOP GOOD HABITS (Deuteronomy 6:5-9). Am I repeatedly acting on positive habits to overcome negative ones?

CHOICE #8—CONTINUALLY CHOOSE THE RIGHT ATTITUDE (Proverbs 3:31). Am I continually choosing to change?

II—The Opportunities Around You:

OPPORTUNITY #1—ENLIST THE COOPERATION OF A GOOD FRIEND (Deuteronomy 32:30). Do I meet regularly with a friend who helps me?

OPPORTUNITY #2—ASSOCIATE WITH THE RIGHT PEOPLE (James 4:4). Are my friends helping or hindering my changes?

OPPORTUNITY #3—SELECT A MODEL TO FOLLOW (Philippians 4:9). Am I spending time with a person I admire?

OPPORTUNITY #4—LEARN FROM YOUR MISTAKES (John 8:11). What recent mistakes have I made which caused me to change?

OPPORTUNITY #5—EXPOSE YOURSELF TO SUCCESSFUL EXPERIENCES (Luke 11:1). What positive event or person will I see today?

III—The God Above You:

STRENGTH #1—GOD'S WORD (2 Timothy 3:16-17). Am I receiving daily strength from God's Word?

STRENGTH #2—PRAYER (James 5:16). Am I praying daily and specifically about my attitude?

STRENGTH #3—THE HOLY SPIRIT (1 John 4:4). Am I continually being filled with the Holy Spirit?

CHRISTIAN HERALD ASSOCIATION AND ITS MINISTRIES

CHRISTIAN HERALD ASSOCIATION, founded in 1878, publishes The Christian Herald Magazine, one of the leading interdenominational religious monthlies in America. Through its wide circulation, it brings inspiring articles and the latest news of religious developments to many families. From the magazine's pages came the initiative for CHRISTIAN HERALD CHILDREN and THE BOWERY MISSION, two individually supported not-for-profit corporations.

CHRISTIAN HERALD CHILDREN, established in 1894, is the name for a unique and dynamic ministry to disadvantaged children, offering hope and opportunities which would not otherwise be available for reasons of poverty and neglect. The goal is to develop each child's potential and to demonstrate Christian compassion and understanding to children in need.

Mont Lawn is a permanent camp located in Bushkill, Pennsylvania. It is the focal point of a ministry which provides a healthful "vacation with a purpose" to children who without it would be confined to the streets of the city. Up to 1000 children between the age of 7 and 11 come to Mont Lawn each year.

Christian Herald Children maintains year-round contact with children by means of a *City Youth Ministry.* Central to its philosophy is the belief that only through sustained relationships and demonstrated concern can individual lives be truly enriched. Special emphasis is on individual guidance, spiritual and family counseling and tutoring. This follow-up ministry to inner-city children culminates for many in financial assistance toward higher education and career counseling.

THE BOWERY MISSION, located at 227 Bowery, New York City, has since 1879 been reaching out to the lost men on the Bowery, offering them what could be their last chance to rebuild their lives. Every man is fed, clothed and ministered to. Countless numbers have entered the 90-day residential rehabilitation program at the Bowery Mission. A concentrated ministry of counseling, medical care, nutrition therapy, Bible study and Gospel services awakens a man to spiritual renewal within himself.

These ministries are supported solely by the voluntary contributions of individuals and by legacies and bequests. Contributions are tax deductible. Checks should be made out either to CHRISTIAN HERALD CHILDREN or to THE BOWERY MISSION.

**Administrative Office: 40 Overlook Drive, Chappaqua, New York 10514
Telephone: (914) 769-9000**

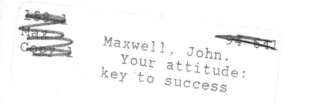
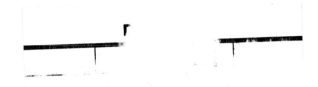